THE NEGLECTED PILLARS:

ELDERS IN RELIGIOUS, HISTORICAL AND LEGAL PERSPECTIVES

Dr. V.R. Uma

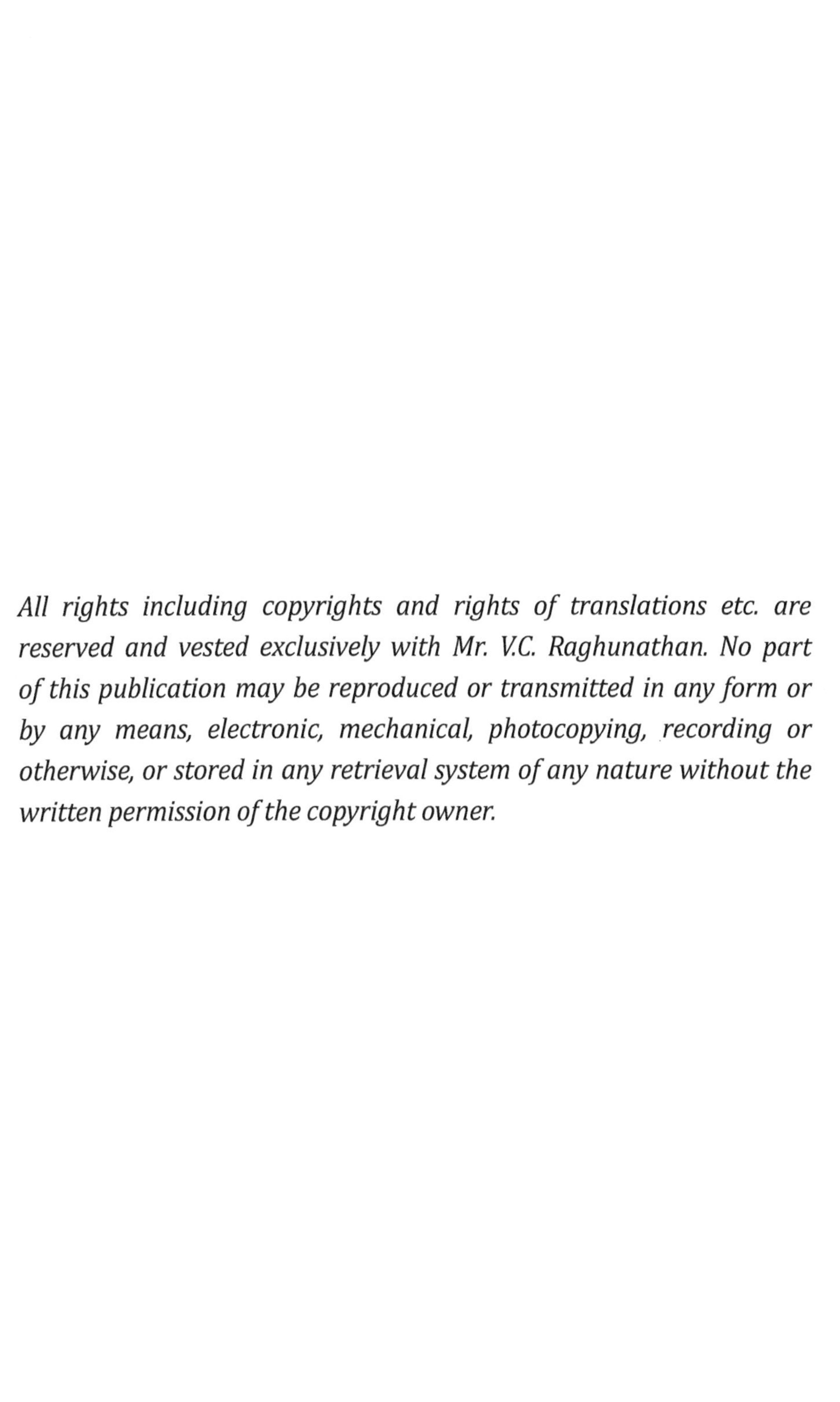

Contents

Part – B: Historical Perspective

Part – C: Legal Perspective

About the Author

DR. V.R. Uma is working as Assistant Professor of Law in DR. Ambedkar Government Law College, Puducherry. The author is the recipient of Gold Medal for having stood as university topper in LL.M. The Author received Prathibha (Meritorious) Award from the Government of Andhra Pradesh in April 2015 for having stood as university topper in LL.M. The author has received two Gold Medals for securing First Rank in Constitutional Law and for securing University First Rank in LL.B. The author has also received Prathibha (Meritorious) Award from the Government of Andhra Pradesh in 2006 for having stood as District Rank holder in her Intermediate (+2) Examination.

The author has started her career as an academician in 2015 and has written several Articles and Chapters in Edited Books. Noteworthy among them are: "Corporate Social Responsibility-Indian Scenario", "Retention of Capital Punishment in India- A Critical Analysis", "Right to Information- A Boon or Bane to India", "Accessibility Issues Relating to Elderly in India- A Study", "Geriatric Health Care Issues in India- Determinants, Challenges and Judicial Intervention", "Senior Citizens and Digital India: Challenges and Opportunities" etc.

The author has done her PhD (Law) on one of the vulnerable groups i.e., senior citizens. A few sections among human beings are, either by nature or because of deep-rooted custom, weak and vulnerable. Among them, senior citizens are one of the most neglected sections of our society. Elderly persons are being increasingly subjected to discrimination and are being isolated by their own kith and kin due to various reasons. This necessitated the Indian Government to draft a special legislation, i.e., Maintenance and Welfare of Parents and Senior Citizens Act, 2007. The author has analysed and has given suggestions for removing the drawbacks and limitations in the 2007 Act so as to make it more effective in obliterating the difficulties faced by the elderly in her Thesis. This book is part of various chapters written by the author in her PhD Thesis.

CHAPTER – 1

General Introduction

1.1. Prelude

Ageing is a natural biological change experienced by all living organisms and human beings are no exception to this. It is the result of the ebbing away of functional capacity of organs and goes hand in hand with deterioration of body structure, functioning of mind and cognizance capacity. No doubt, this results in lot of challenges to the ageing people in everyday life. It is witnessed that the demography of the world population is changing fast due to numerous reasons. In 2020, the population of senior citizens of more than 60years old was more than of that of children below 5 years. The great leaps in the health care sciences have resulted in the increased longevity and thus the surge in the elderly population. While the population of elderly was 12% in the year 2015, it is expected to almost double up to 22%, in the year 2050[1]. In fact, there is no typical elderly person. Lakhs of elderly manage their ageing issues like curtailment of physical activities and cognitive changes constructively and successfully. They also cope with the bereavements that are a part of late life. A successful ageing depends upon three factors such as absence of ailments and body impairments, continuance of cognizance ability and maintaining a social life.

---

1   NSO (2021), Elderly in India, National Statistical Office, Ministry of Statistics and Programme Implementation, Government of India, New Delhi.

The pace of modern life style, which is miles ahead to that of elders inching into their sunset years, has resulted in the loss of human touch. It is compounded by the changing social and traditional values that have widened the generation gap and further leading to fissures in our social fabric. It is normal for the aged people to have their own set of yearnings, hopes and expectations from their kith and kin and society. A kind of insecurity and uncertainty are developed when these hopes are not met with. These insecurities and uncertainty may exist in different forms and may be cloaked in various masks but they nevertheless exist. With the breakneck pace of the modern life, the younger generation is found neglecting their elders without a whit of concern and relegate the latter to the side lines at home. The neglect is in forms of isolation, desertion and social alienation. There is a plethora of evidences of physical and mental abuse, violations of human, statuary and healthcare rights, exclusion from decision making, deprivation of their choices, social status etc... Often, they are reduced to financial dependency on the youngsters.

Indian and other eastern cultures are known for their filial duty and all the major religions insist on this moral duty. Filial duty encompasses treating the elders with love, affection, empathy, respect, esteem, honour and reverence. The duty of taking care of parents and elders is imbibed in the Indian tradition and culture. Even mythological stories which date back to many millennium years have emphasised the filial responsibility of the children in taking care of the aged people and have given a spiritual colour to the said duty. It is said that the filial duty is the reciprocation of the love, care, support and attention they have received from their parents during their childhood. In other words, the filial duty is an equitable exchange of love though the filial duty is no match for the parental love. It can also be argued that the filial duty is a result of the warmth, love, affection, and compassion towards the debilitating parents rather than a reciprocatory affection or a social debt. Another contention is that the warm, heartfelt, affectionate and emotional as well as intergenerational bond that the children feel towards their parents culminates in taking care of the latter during their dotage years. However, it is sad to note the much cherished and adored traditional and moral duty is witnessing a rapid decline across all societies and countries. The discernable drift towards abandonment, neglect and isolation is witnessed more during economic downturns, famines, social calamities, pandemics etc... It was heart rending to watch the elders were being deserted during the calamitous covid-19 period. There are many aspects that chipped in to the neglect of the aged such as changes in the family structure from joint family system that transposed into nuclear families, industrialisation, migration, increased longevity, decreasing birth rates etc... The increase in the number of women workforces, who were the traditional care takers of the aged, is also another crucial reason. Ill-treatment, dereliction, intolerance and disrespect towards the elders have always been there during all the times. Different forms of abuse are hard to severalise since they are persistent in our collective consciousness. A less benevolent and a more exigent society had always been more abusive of elders. Progress in civilisation and economic advancements have not been any barriers for ill-treatment of elders.

1.2. Filial and Elderly Care Under Various Cultures

It was a common perception among us that people during ancient times became old at a very young age. Another misconception is that they used to die at a young age, if not during their youth. Historical evidences suggest that people, at least some individuals, lived far long enough than the people of modern times. In classical western literatures, pseudo-historical persons are credited to have lived for three to four centuries. And mythical characters Sibyls and Tithonus were alive for many centuries.[2] King of Pylos, Nestor, was said to have lived for three hundred years. During the days of Genesis, people are said have lived longer than hundred years. Even in Hinduism, sage Thirumoolar was said to have lived for more than three thousand years. Sages like Agasthiyar, Bhogar and his disciples lived for many centuries. During Dwaparayug, it has been said that, people lived over two hundred years. Despite rapid advances in modern health care system and the developments in the field of medicine and in spite of demographic change in the last century, people in modern times do not live longer than what they did during the past historical period. There has not been any significant increase in the life span of people for the last three millennia. But the percentage of people who are able to survive into old age increased dramatically during the last two centuries due to the advances in the medical field.

The term old age is at best a social construct than a specific biological phase or point of life. It is difficult to demarcate the exact point at which a colour band in a rainbow changes into another colour band for there is no clear cut boundary line between colour

---

2   Status of Older People: The Ancient and Biblical Worlds, available at: <https://www.encyclopedia.com/education/encyclopedias-almanacs-transcripts-and-maps/status-older-people-ancient-and-biblical-worlds> (last accessed on May 08, 2025).

bands in a rainbow. Similarly, there is no suggestion to indicate when the old age begins. It is accepted that the middle age gives birth to old age, but when? From the biological point of view, the exact age where from the old age starts depend upon the society, culture and even history. Till the last millennia during which medical advancements were practically very little, the average life span of the people was less than 60 years. There is always a social stigma about the old age and elderly right from ancient period, especially in western world. It is sad and surprising to note the equivocation and ambiguity among various cultures about the role of elders. It was thought they were either a source of wisdom or a phase of decrepit and frail which do not contribute anything to the society. To have a better perception about the role of elders in our society, it is imperative to have knowledge of how the elders were treated during various periods of time in the past. It is often said that, it is a requisite to know the past before we start to think where we would like to be in future. Such an understanding would lead on a path to an age-inclusive society which is necessary. How the elders were treated in various cultures in the past – during ancient and medieval periods – in various cultures and religions in India is discussed in this book. The significance given to older persons in various religions that were practiced during various periods of history and during the rule of different dynasties in India and also the legislative measures taken for protecting the rights of senior citizens after India attaining independence till the present day are discussed in this book very briefly.

1.2.1. Classical Greek and Roman Cultures

Literature, scripts and historical evidences clearly have pointed out that elders were treated with reverence in the classical past and there existed a 'golden age' during which they enjoyed primacy and had great influence in religious, social and political spheres. Those societies which followed traditional beliefs and had a robust oral tradition, the elderly people were the storehouse of culture and wisdom. History is replete with the list of elders, during the ancient period, who held sway in all fields of everyday life like politics, literature, philosophy and religion. Of course, it was a mixed bag for them since literature provides us with both good and bad images of old age. Attitude and impression that one gets from these evidence suggest opinion about elders were both genial and acerbic. During the period of Aristotle, the people of Athens treated the elders with derision and contempt and used to rebel against their opinions. Old age was often associated with debilitation and was considered atrophied while adolescence, handsomeness and vitality were greatly appreciated.[3] In ancient Greek, people were persuaded to take care of their parents since it was their legal obligation. Those who have not fulfilled their filial duty were barred from contesting for public offices. During sixth century, a negligent Athenian who has forsaken his parents was likely to lose his citizenship. However, in ancient Sparta, southern part of present Greece, had a powerful governing body, Gerousia. It was a council of elders which had powers over the larger assembly on many issues. It acted as a criminal court for serious crimes. Seniors in age were first allowed to express their views in the council. Sparta was an exception and stood out among the rest of Europe's tradition of derision, contempt and impertinence towards senior citizens.[4]

---

3   Chris Gilleard, "Old Age in Ancient Greece: narratives of desire, narrative of disgust" 21 Journal of Ageing Studies 84 (2007).

4   Christopher M. Bellitto, Honoring the elderly: A cautionary tale from Ancient Greece, available at: <https://www.northjersey.com/story/opinion/contrib utors/2017/03/20/honoring-elderly-cautionary-tale-ancient-greece> (last accessed on May 08, 2025).

1.2.2. European Culture

In Europe, the documentations aver that the old age alone was not the reason for they had been bestowed with command and power over others. The age factor alone did not automatically enable or elevate them to a status that demanded deference and reverence. Scores of evidences suggest that opulence and authority were in the control of youngsters in most instances. It was the individual's flair to function as an active member of the society decided his status in the society. It was true for all people in sections of society. Be he a king, aristocrat, noble, business man or common man, it was his ability to remain active as an important part of the society that decided his place in the society. Most of them had a life expectancy below 50 years and very few reached the age of 70 and above. The healthy individual who reached 40 years was respected. However, those who were sick and frail were treated with disdain, looked down and even killed. Often, the term 'old age' was related to lack of ability to be productive to the society. The care for the elders rested with the children or relatives in absence of welfare state. Even in the case affluent individual elders, it was not of any great difference except that they did not depend on others for bare survival. They also considered the old age a period which was to be an endured rather than a period of jollity in the evening of their life. Even in democratic Athens, old age alone did not beget leadership or authority. And in Rome, it was stated that power rested with middle aged senators, irrespective of the fact whether the king was old or young. Liabilities of old age were suspiciously viewed and were considered a risk to confer authority to old men.

During ancient times, in Europe, it was sometimes thought that old age itself was a disease. However saner minds were also prevailed saying that ageing is a natural process. However, it must be noted that old age was not viewed genially in European literature also. Marginalisation of old women as sex-crazed and alcoholics witches was not uncommon. They, who were in their past reproduction stages, were derisively treated as non functioning members of the society. However, men in their old age were treated less disdainfully than women, though it was not seen in a positive attitude. It was not viewed as an inalienable phase of life that one has to pass through during his full life cycle. Most men of old age continued to work till their demise. For destitute sections of the society, who could not support by themselves, old age would have been a double whammy. There was an old saying, "old age and poverty are burdensome, but in combination they are impossible to bear". Those penurious people would have endured a desolated old age, if they had been deserted by their children. Filial obligation, as in classical Athens, would have been an oasis in the desert, but might not have reached out to women. For affluent sections of the society, old age would not have been bothersome as long as help in the form of slaves were available. Cicero, the Greek philosopher, was unerring when he said "Old age will only be respected if it fights for itself, maintains its rights, avoids dependence on anyone, and asserts control over its own to the last breath." Sometimes, in spite of the negativism that is associated with it, ageing and old age were considered natural phases of human life. In Europe, during Medieval and Renaissance periods also, the elders were either treated condescendingly and put to death or honoured depending on the circumstances or habits of the society. During the 16th century, the Europe was such a cruel society that some of them asked the elders to live an isolated decrepit life or to meet an honourable death.

1.2.3. Mediterranean and Latin Culture

The treatment meted out to the elders was on par with that of Asian countries. Elders were responsible for the general maintenance of the family. Elders were fully assimilated into the family structure, with no inhibitions.

1.2.4. Eastern Hemisphere

Eastern cultural thinking was opposite to that of western world during all periods of time. Family was viewed as the basic unit of the society and elders were venerated as the head of such a family. Filial piety was the norm in all civilized countries in this part of the world. Elders were treated with honour and due respect. Their wisdom was much solicited in all spheres of life. Be it India, China, Sri Lanka, Indonesia, Japan etc...the elders were much revered. Even the aborigines in Australia honoured their elders for millennia.

1.2.5. Indian Culture

Various cultures have different perceptions on ageing and death. And these attitudes can cause different experiences of growing older. In Indian tradition, ageing is not limited to biological process alone. It is also a cultural one. In some parts of India, death is even celebrated since the soul is liberated from the earthly worries. Hindu philosophy postulates that the earthly life is only an interregnum and a dream. The mores of the concept of filial piety vary according to culture and way of living. While eastern cultures have great respect and honour for their elders, they are sidelined from the society in western culture and thus rendering ageing a shameful experience. Culture of Indians, Koreans native American Indians, Chinese, Japanese etc... venerate their elders.

India's intellectual contribution to this world is unparalleled. History is replete with evidences of India imparting knowledge to the world in every field of life, along with its esoteric philosophy in the form of debates. It is a country of humungous knowledge gained over many millennia by the sages and saints that are shared with the common man. Indian culture emphasizes the exquisite connection between the perceptible features of life to its intangible strands. The penumbras of personal, spiritual and social aspects of life are thoroughly and explicitly explained.

Part – A

Religious Perspective

CHAPTER – 2

Filial and Elderly Care in India – Religious Perspective

Introduction

The Indian social matrix is very complex in nature to a foreigner. This land has witnessed ancient civilisations as old as 5000 years old. Some contest that it is much older than what the western historiographers care to agree. It is a land where four major religions of the world viz Hinduism, Buddhism, Jainism and Sikhism were born and co exist with a religious tolerance seen nowhere in this world. Also alien religions along with their cultures like Islam, Christianity and Judaism have also taken their roots here. Added to this and as a result of assimilation of some other cultures like Bahai, Yahudi, Parsians, etc..., the Indian way of life got coloured under the influence and shadows of these traditions, cults and cultures[1]. It is not far from the truth to call the contemporary lifestyle of an average Indian is the conglomeration of all these traditions. Thus the social structure and culture have become extremely complex.

A society's prosperity and way of living altered the perception, both positive and negative, it has on old age and the people belonging to this section. This is true irrespective of the time period, whether ancient, medieval or modern. The culture and the values associated the society are also the deciding factors in the above perception. A

---

1   S. C. Tiwari and Nisha M. Pandey, "The Indian concepts of lifestyle and mental health in old age", 55 *Indian Journal of Psychiatry* 288 – 292 (2013).

culture followed by a segment or society of people can be broadly and loosely defined as a way of living. A way of living is the behaviour, habits etc that are followed by the society. And it keeps changing with times. It is not cast in stone. Even if it is cast in stone as in Ten Commandments, as time evolves and progresses, it does not stand as a permanent fixture. Way of living is largely governed by principles of the religion that the people follow. These religious principles are drawn from the preaching of its founders and proponents, as in the case of Abrahamic religions – Judaism, Christianity and Islam or Buddhism or Jainism. Those preaching are compiled in the form of Holy Books. In case of Hinduism, since there is no founder, the way of living is drawn from Vedic texts, Smritis, Shrutis, Upanishads and Puranas. A particular way of living practised for long enough becomes a tradition or custom of that segment or society. Also a tradition gets influenced by the newer interpretations of religious principles and Holy books. It is not uncommon in all religions that there have been numerous intercalations and insertions in the Holy books. For example, in Manu Smritis, many of its enunciated principles are said to be later additions of vested interests. These additions or insertions or interpretations influence and alter the customs, either for good or bad, of the society. For example, sati was a much venerated horrendous tradition during medieval period which no longer exists in the modern society. Religious terrorism, which was not much in existence during the last century, is the biggest predicament of the society now. Hence it can be inferred that religion shapes the basic attitude and customs of its people. The perception of the society is influenced by the principles of the religion. Way of living of the society governed by the teachings in the religion. Tradition may change with time, as said earlier, for various reasons. But the basic principles of all religions remain intact, unaffected by vortex of changes of time.

Love, truth, honesty, sympathy, and empathy for elders are some of the constituent tenets of all religions which have never been questioned by the later interpreters. These persuasions have never been put on the examination table. May be their importance had been eclipsed for a short while, but they do regain their rightful centre place once the veil covering them gets removed. Thus, religion has become the cornerstone of way of living or tradition or customs of the society. How a society behaved during a particular period can be deduced from the religion it followed and the principles that existed during that time. In this context, it becomes relevant to examine the status of elders and parents in various religions that were practiced during various times. In ancient India, Hinduism, Buddhism and Jainism were the major religions that were competing with each other to garner the support of the people. During medieval times, Islam and Christianity have gained prominence in different parts of India. The preaching of each religion on devotion and deference to be shown on parents, elders and teachers has been discussed in this part.

2.1. **Filial and Elderly Care in Hinduism**

It has been ingeminated many times by innumerable number of scholars that Hinduism is more than just a religion. It is a culture, a way of life, a behavioural code, built upon age old customs, beliefs, traditions, family ties and social values. And that's the reason Hindus use a different word to describe their religion – Sanatana Dharma, which means eternal faith, or the eternal way things are (truth), or eternal path or eternal order. Among many other principles, the Hinduism is based on two main concepts. The first concept is belief in the law of karma (cause and effect of your deeds) and rebirth. The second is the concept of liberation (moksha) by which a relief from the countless and endless cycles of rebirth and hence from samsara is made possible. A unique feature of Hinduism is that it is a compilation of many traditions and philosophies. It is a Dharmic religion and the word Dharmic has several meanings. It means duty, virtue, morality, righteousness and religion, depending upon the context and these precepts lay down the fundamental principles of righteous conduct. Hinduism strongly reiterates that the universe is sustained by Dharma. It upholds the culture and moral values and makes the nature to function in a pre-determined path.

Hinduism is considered to be eternal and it is more a way of living than a religion. It resolutely believes that there is God in every matter, whether living or not. Love, kindness, sympathy and empathy are the hall marks of Hinduism. When a person hails another saying "Namasthe" with folded hands, it is said that he is greeting the second person as well as 'Shiva", the omnipresent God inside him. That is the reason a Hindu seeks permission from the plant to pluck flowers from it. And this is the reason why he seeks permission and earnestly prays the insects to migrate to a different safer place when ground breaking ceremony is conducted.

According to Hinduism, God is omnipresent and so is considered to be present in everything, in all forms of lives and objects. This is the secret behind treating everyone with love and respect leading a joyous and contended life. The Hinduism and Indian civilization is an assemblage and confluence of maturity and spiritualism. The scholarly and earnest civilization, known for its sagacity is still continuing its unchallenged sway over the contemporary life style and thoughts. And it is the longest surviving civilization in spite of many wars, subjugation, varied foreign cultural onslaughts, colonisation etc... and there exists a much appreciated continuum of its culture from faraway past of many millenniums back to present[2]. The ancient Indian civilization still has a strong influence on the present day Hindu culture and life style. This is the longest surviving society, formed from that civilization, from millenniums of years back, still evolving, keeping pace with time and most importantly in sync with time. The other equally renowned civilizations have vanished into thin air without a trace of them for the simple reason that they refused to change with time. Hinduism, which is entwined with the Indian civilization, with its flexible philosophy about everything in this universe is the reason for this sustainability.

Unlike the other Dharmic religions that are born in India, viz Buddhism, Jainism or Sikhism – that also believe Moksha is the most supreme state of the atman (soul) and other major religions like Christianity and Islam, Hinduism has no any historical founder. The large body of Sacred texts – Vedas, Upanishads,18 Puranas, Maha Kavyas (Ramayan and Mahabharat) – state the way of righteous living, ways of worship, governing rituals among many other rules

---

2   Ala Narayana and Saketh Ram Thrigulla, "Geriatric health Care – A historical Perspective", 28 *Bulletin of the Indian Institute of History of Medicine, Hyderabad* 1-19 (2007).

and provide the necessary authority. The oldest of the texts, the Vedas may date back more than four thousand years. Vedas are believed to have been written down during Vedic period. However, another school of thought believes that they have been existing from even much earlier period and are passed on orally through guru-shisya parampa. The texts in Vedas are mostly verses, hymns and ritual treatises that are mostly instructional and are written in the ancient Indian language, Sanskrit. They contain revelations from God/Bramhan, as received by ancient saints and sages. Hindus revere Vedas since they strongly believe that the Vedas are the bedrock of their culture and regard them as eternal revelations. The Vedas reveal what is Dharma, and Dharma is that which ennobles a person, makes him a virtuous and righteous person, a person of values. The Vedic texts offer an insight into life. It understood the people and their motivations in a precise manner that a modern day psychologist would never assume. And that is the reason, they always have a solution for every problem that the people face. And it always offered a correctional path whenever the humans erred. Always directing us to a dharmic path in sync with the universe. The construct of right and wrong, in Hinduism, centres on the moral compass of Vedic texts and Holy scriptures. The much venerated fundamental teachings and ideas of Hinduism are contained in the concluding portion of the Vedas and they are the most recent part of them and are therefore known as the Vedanta (the concluding portion of the Vedas" or object, the highest purpose of Veda). These are more widely known as the Upanishads which teach meditation, philosophy and metaphysics while other parts of Vedas deal with mantras, rituals, ceremonies and sacrifice. Upanishads played a major role in the shift or transition from Vedic ritualism to new thoughts, concepts and philosophies in Hinduism and are considered as the most important in Hindu religion, Hindu culture and Hindu literature and remain as the spiritual core of Hinduism. There are said to be around 108 Upanishads.

The cultural significance and perception about old age is somewhat refracted among the Hindus, whereas it is largely coloured among those who are foreign to this land by birth and culture. The duties of the elders during this phase of life have been explicitly enunciated in the 'Dharmasastras' and 'Dharmasutras' and the greatest epics, the'Ramayana' and the 'Mahabharat' and the 18 Puranas. Where the former denotes the treatises about the concept of 'Dharma', the latter speaks about the appropriate rules that have to be followed by a human being. Viewing of Hinduism through coloured lenses by a foreigner starts from the very interpretation of the word 'Dharma'. The word takes different meanings that are appropriate to the context in which it is placed. It acquires the meanings such as duty, justice, character, nature, characteristics, behaviour etc... The meaning depends upon the milieu in which it is discussed. These texts have enunciated the ideal life course for every human being. Over and above that, these ancient texts have articulated in detail the cultural significance and meanings attached to the natural process of aging. Some authors allude that this life course model is suggested for upper caste males only[3] though there is nothing in the texts to substantiate such innuendos. It must be noted that the issues were implicitly discussed from the female perspective also. The roles and responsibilities of each human being to be followed by every Hindu is clearly delineated in its Ashram Dharma and is common for all, including the both the genders though it is not specifically mentioned. This Dharma is an age based social system. It is believed by the practitioners of

---

3   Usha Menon , "Old Age and Hinduism", 1 Oxford Bibliographies 83 (2018).

The Ashram Dharma that it leads them into the fulfilment of the four aims of life, namely Dharma (righteousness), Artha (wealth), Kama (desires and passions) and Moksha (salvation). The total life period of every one human life is divided into four stages.[4] It is believed that the Lord, MahaVishnu, himself has explained the salient features of the concept of Varnashrama Dharma. Here, Dharma means righteousness and He enunciated the basic tenants of virtuous conduct.

1. *Brahmacharya (celibate student hood) :*

    The person lives with spiritual guru and practices strict celibacy. The person learns Vedas and other spiritual texts during this stage. He is to serve his guru and is made to live on alms through begging which teaches him humility. He is to observe a strict moral restraint.

2. *Grahastha (House holder stage) :*

    The person enters into this stage after Brahmacharya. He leads a life of samsara and seeks artha (money) and kama (bodily pleasure). He is to raise a family and fulfil the duties towards his society. He is permitted to earn money and enjoy sensual pleasures within the framework of morality. His duties are worship, keep the sacred fire at his home burning all the time, donating alms to the brahmcharis of the earlier stage of life, spiritual gurus and saints, feed the destitute and animals, teach his children morality and spirituality etc. The Grahastha is the benefactor to the people in other three stages of life.

---

4   Kurma Purana, available at: <http://hinduonline.co/Scriptures/Puranas/ KurmaPurana.html> (last accessed on May 04, 2025).

3. *Vanasprastha (forest dwelling stage / Hermitage):*

The person, with his wife, leaves for forest, turns his attention towards his inner self and engages in spiritual practices, religious rites, meditation and prayer. This stage is a precursor for the next stage when he makes attempts to achieve self-realization. He leads a simple life style surviving on fruits and roots and his relationship with his off springs is no more than being a mentor. Both husband and wife retreat to a secluded and quieter place for deeper spiritual practices.

4. *Sanyasa (Hermithood):*

During this final stage, the person further retreats from worldly engagements and involvements. All his ties with his earlier stages of lives are cut off. They live on food received by begging. They try to realise the true nature of atman or attain, as a yogi, supreme wisdom through intense meditation.

Ashrama Dharma, as said earlier, is age specific and it endows a Hindu to enjoy the life goals of a Hindu, called Purusartha viz Dharma, Artha, Kama and Moksha in a time specific manner. A strict period of celibacy and discipline are enforced during the first stage so as to train the person in puritanical self-abnegation, forbearance and responsibility which will help him during his later years of life. During Grahastha stage, the person involves in sensual pleasures for procreation through which the life in this world is sustained without any breaks. He is also allowed to pursue wealth. However, he is restrained to enjoy the pleasures of Artha and Kama within the confines of morality. All these desires are justifiable and are valid and are regarded with due respect. The mark of a full life is the extent to which the person has allowed these desires to flourish during the appropriate stages. This stage wise fulfilment of duties and desires asserts the theory that a person is ready for a specific stage when he is ripe for that stage. Fulfilments of righteous duties, accumulation of wealth and to revel sensual delights are age specific and these doctrines function both on horizontal and vertical levels. During the first level, the person is bound by worldly duties, performing them according to his age spreading across half his life term. And during the later level, his interest in this worldly chores wanes and starts his journey towards ultimate destination – moksha. This can be viewed, depending upon the prism through which one looks, either as emancipation from the sufferings of cycles of birth and death and confined to a finite form or merge with the Supreme Being. Thus a Hindu is always dynamic and sprightly throughout his life. Since the person is uncoupled from worldly commitments, Vanaprastha and Sanyasa are considered as detachment stages. Alternatively, "a withdrawal on the horizontal level is the starting point of his journey on the vertical level". All the energies obtained during his training during the Bramhacharya are reserved for the final stage. Hinduism views life as continuous and gradational realization of self, athman, validating ashram dharma. It solemnly asserts its faith in man believing that he is filled with dignity, capable of performing his duties to society, nature and Brahman, to meet his karmic debts thereby advance into his journey to moksha, This is in total contrast with the western moral systems, claiming to be realistic models, believes in the decadence and depravity of man. Some authors are of the opinion that as per Hindu tradition old age as a period of differential, but not total disengagement.[5] Generally, the old age is considered an

---

5   Tilak Shrinivas, "Religion and Aging in the Indian Tradition" 35 State University of New York Press 65 (1989).

opportunity for cultivating renunciation.[6] The opportune time of practicing world renunciation depends upon the richness of life being renounced.

Vedas emphasize that devotion to elders is equivalent to devotion to God. In spite of the common perception, the Vedas do not claim or demand anything from the practitioners of Hinduism. Actually Vedas does not propound any theory to be followed by anyone. Vedas enlightens what is Dharma or Adharma and simply elucidates what makes a person to be ennobled as a dharmic person. The Vedas do not coerce or urge anyone to adhere to any principle. But it glorifies the person who abides by the Dharmic principles. Care and compassion for the parents is a Dharma and hence the Vedas much revere the warm feelings towards the parents. The Vedas suggest that parents should be considered as God, Ishwara in form of a human. This principle is so sacred, so fundamental, so revered, that it is reiterated many times in our Vedic texts. Parents have to be regarded, revered, looked after and interacted as though they were Ishwara, since they were the reason for his existence. It's a way of showing gratitude for the hardships they have encountered for his upbringing. Such emotion will make the person compassionate and helps the person to develop devotion to the God which will make it easier to attain the ultimate goal of salvation. Also, it mentally prepares the person to face the twilight of his own life with equanimity.

A critical part of Hindu tradition is to respect the elders irrespective of the fact whether he is related or not. A younger person is required to offer pranams (obeisance, prostration or bowing forward) whenever he meets an elder person. It is done

---

6   Ram Prasad Chakravarthi, "A Classical Indian Philosophical Perspective on Ageing and the Meaning of Life" 15 Ageing and Society 1-36 (1995).

in order to show honour and respect towards elderly people like parents, grandparents, elderly relatives, teachers and saints. This innate behaviour is an essential part of the Hindu culture and children are repeatedly taught of this norm in India. The Hindu culture is an embodiment of reverence to elders. Showing respect is the very fabric of Hindu culture and has no social boundaries. To love and take care of parents, there is no requirement that they were picture perfect human beings or ideal parents, for every human being is filled with flaws. The traditional norms and values of the Indian society emphasize on the duty of taking care of elders. Hindu culture emphasises that duties of children towards one's parent are a debt owed to them. This care towards the parents is more culturally based rather than development dependent, irrespective of the status of the person. Various Hindu texts, Kavyas and scriptures have repeatedly and strongly emphasized the importance of these duties. In Kurma Purana, one of the eighteen Mahapuranas named after Lord Vishnu in His tortoise avatar, a great emphasis has been laid on the importance of treating parents and elders with reverence and is believed that Lord himself has explained this conduct to sage Naradha.

> *"The father, mother, teacher, elder brother and one's provider – these five are considered as one's superiors" – Kurma Purana 2.12.32*

> *"He who desires prosperity should revere these superiors at all times by all means, even if he loses his life" – Kurma Purana 2.12.33*

> *"The son should be devoted to them and make their care his first priority" – Kurma Purana 2.12.34b*

"No Deva can equal the mother, and no superior can equal one's father. Hence, no son can get relieved of the debt he owes to them" – Kurma Purana 2.12.36

Taittiriya Upanishad, a Vedic era text in Sanskrit, is part of Yajurveda. It is one of the 108 Upanishads and is listed as 7th in the Muktika canon of 108 Upanishads. Apart from prayers and benedictions, it offers advice, from the Guru, on ethics and morals to students who are set to leave their gurukul after completion of their studies. The eleventh anuvaka of Shiksha Valli list behavioural guidelines for the graduating students as follows:

"Be one to whom a mother is as god, be one to whom a father is as god,

Be one to whom an Acharya (spiritual guide, scholars you learn from) is as god, be one to whom a guest is as god.

Let your actions be uncensurable, none else.

Those acts that you consider good when done to you, do those to others, none else"[7]

The meaning of this verse is that one should revere, honour and serve his mother, father, guests including the destitute and those who are in dire straits and guru before worshipping God. In other words, the scriptures place these people a step ahead of God and emphasise the importance of serving the elders. This is in complete contrast with the principles of non-Dharmic religions which place God above everyone and everything. In Hindu culture, mother is the most respected person, followed by father, more than even God.

---

7   Taittiriya Upanishad 1.11.2, available at: <https://gita.pub/upanishad/taittiriya/verse/1-11-2> (last accessed on May 05, 2025).

The importance and significance of obeying and revering the parents, elders and guru have been enunciated in Manusmrithi also. It is said to have been written between 2nd Century BCE and 3rd century CE by sages Manu and Bhirgu. However considerable divergent opinions are there over the authenticity of the author(s) and the period. It covers a wide range of topics like duties, conduct and rights of persons belonging to various castes, laws governing them, virtuous and righteous behaviours of all people. It is believed by many that it is one of the ancient legal texts among the many Dharmasastras. Also, it is one of the most misquoted and misunderstood ancient texts. It is feared that many insertions found their way to the original text and the authenticity of the texts available now is questionable. The texts have defined duties of a son to his parents elaborately. It says that:

"No person can repay his parents even in 100 years for all the troubles that they go through to give birth to him and raise him to adulthood. Therefore, always try to do whatever pleases your parents and your teacher, because only then any religious worship done by you will bear any fruit" – Manusmrithi 2.227 – 228

"He who serves his parents and teachers truly respects all the teachings of the scriptures. And the person who disrespects them will never get the fruit of any worship" – Manusmrithi 2.234

"Therefore, as long as they are alive, no one should devote himself to any other religious undertaking. Rather, he should continue to serve them with full diligence and do whatever pleases them and is beneficial to them" – Manusmrithi 2.235

"In fact, by serving one's parents and teachers, a person fulfils all his major religious duties. Other religious acts like worshiping are minor, compared to serving these elders" – Manusmrithi 2.237

"For one who is in the habit of saluting and constantly revering elders,—four things prosper: viz., longevity, merit, fame and strength" – Manusmrithi 121

"All the duties have been honoured by him who has honoured these three; and all acts remain fruitless for him who does not honour them" – Manusmrithi 234

"So long as these three live, he should not do anything else; he should always render service unto them, rejoicing in what is pleasing and beneficial to them" – Manusmrithi 235

"He should communicate to them by thought, word or deed whatever he may do without injury to them, for the sake of the next life" –Manusmrithi 236

"All that ought to be done by man is finished on these three; this is the highest direct duty; every other is a subordinate duty" – Manusmrithi 237

"The service of these three is declared to be the highest austerity; until permitted by them, one should not perform any other meritorious act" – Manusmrithi 229

"The preceptor, the father, the mother and the elder brother should not be treated with disrespect, especially by a Brāhman, even though he is distressed" – Manusmrithi 225

"One who serves the Elderly is adored by even Rakshasas" – Manusmrithi VII/38

"The elders should not be insulted" Chapter IV 1141

"Quarreling with elders should be avoided" – Chapter IV1179,180

"A king should forgive litigants, infants, elders and sick people" – Chapter VIII 1312

"A king should show patience with the following persons and treat them kindly; aged Brahman, sick persons, distressed persons, infants, elders, indigent people" – Chapter VIII1395

In addition to Manusmrithi, there are various other texts, supposedly written by various sages expounding the importance of showing reverence to the aged section of the society.

i. *Apasthambha Dharma Sutras:*

They form a section of Kalpa sutras. It is based on Yajur Veda and elucidates the duties and sacrifices to be performed by the first three section of the society. It says that,

"A student need to pray before the morning meal and show reverence to the aged at his dwelling place (Prasana 1, Patala2, Khandas/13)"

ii. *Gautama Dharma Sutras:*

It is said to be one of the earliest Dharmasutras and has 1000 aphorisms placed in 28 chapters. It can be called as the oldest law book for Hindus. It discloses various dharmas to be followed by all the sections of the people, in accordance with their placement in the society. It spells out the duties of a king, breaks down the punishment for offences of all kinds, deciphers the funeral rites, reveals the food habits to be followed, elucidates the dharmas to be followed by women gender, expounds the rules on succession of property and not to be left behind, render the rules on atonement for sins. It seems to be an exhaustive rule book covering various topics in everyday life of a Hindu. It demands a person to do the following;

"Before having his own meal, a person must feed his guests, make sure infants, physically indisposed and pregnant women have been fed. Also he should make sure that the womenfolk and elderly persons are also had their food" (Chapter Y 25)

iii. *Vasishta Dharma Sutras:*

It exhorts a person to give way when he encounters the following people. Elderly persons, infants, ailing people, those carrying load, females and those travelling in chariots. – Chapter XIII 5S

When faced with conflicting documents on issues like property, it directs that statements of aged inhabitants shall be given more weightage among others – Chapter XVL 15

A king should not levy tax on the following persons. An aged Brahman, his own attendant, one who has no guardian, sanyasi, a child, aged persons and a student – Chapter XIX 23

iv. *Baudhayana Dharma Sutras:*

These sutras prohibit a combatant from fighting with, those who are afraid, tipsy, mentally retarded, unarmed persons, women, infants, Brahman and aged persons (Prasna I, Adyaya 10, Kandika IS/II)

No other philosophy other than Hinduism has provided such varied spiritual instructions to take care of the parents and elders and thereby attain the Supreme Truth or Lord. The metaphysical nature of thought process of Hinduism enables such practical training. In Hindu culture, such spiritual training and instructions originate from the elders, often from the family itself. Hence, the relationship between the elders of the family and the younger generation transcends beyond the mutual love, affection and trust. A spiritual bond and relationship, that is unheard of in the western hemisphere, is formed between them. Thus, the elders in the family are treated with utmost reverence. Such respect is expressed and reflected in the form of following etiquette, decorum and behaviour while in the vicinity of the aged people.

They are to be received by standing up.

They are never to be called by their first name. They should be addressed by the conventional titles of papa, mama, grandpa, uncle etc... If situation warrants when addressing elderly strangers, the word 'ji' ,which denotes respect, should be added with their surnames or first names.

Younger generation has to maintain an upright sitting or standing posture in the company of elders. Leg over leg sitting, feet stretching towards the elders, hands clapped behind the head are considered as impolite, rude and discourteous to aged people.

Smoking and drinking alcohol in the company of elders are viewed as most disrespectful.

> Speaking to them with raised voice and showing blatant anger, using abusive language and usage of impersonal words are considered as rude
>
> When talking to an elder, one should always look towards the elder person. Looking towards other directions or rotating one's head or eyes while talking to an elder are considered rude and disrespectful.

There are many more such etiquettes that have to be followed before elders. The young children have to keep their hands in front of their mouth while speaking to elders as a gesture of respect. Humility while in the company of elders is mandatory. The Vedic texts and scriptures affirm that humility is a strength not a weakness. Similarly pride is considered a weakness, not as strength. And humility leads to right thinking and right living.

Great emphasis has also has been laid on the reverence and care that should be taken towards a guru, teacher. A guru is one who imparts knowledge to someone. The religious texts say that parents-in-law and grandparents are also have to considered as guru amongst many others. It once again stresses that these people, including his parents, have to treated with respect, taken care of and served at all costs. It is reiterated that those children who show deference and serve their parents are rewarded in life and those who do not will be subjected to bad karma. A person who neglects his duty to his parents is unlikely to be answered for his prayers by the God. This concept has been explained with the help of the story, in the epic Mahabharat, of a young saint Kousika who gets involved in Tapas and meditation, disregarding the needs of his aged parents. He was of the opinion that spiritual advancement and salvation are more important than his dharmic duty of taking care of his parents.

However, he finds to his dismay, bewilderment and wonder, that an ordinary woman who was painstakingly meticulous in following her household dharma and a butcher who was very diligent in taking care of his aged parents were more spiritually advanced than the young saint. The butcher Dharma Vyadha explains to the young saint that serving the parents alone results in greater spiritual reward and relinquishing the duties, as a son, towards his parents does not lead to salvation. Similar thoughts have been reiterated in the following texts.

"The son who pleases his parents by his good qualities acquires the fruit of all good virtues" – Kurma Purana 2.12.35

"Service to one's parents is the only essence of Dharma and it leads one to Moksha upon death" – Kurma Purana 2.12.38b

There is another story of Pundalika in the town of Pandharpur who doted on his parents, devoted to them, and was taking great care of them. He took immense pleasure in serving them. Lord told his wife that Pundalika has been worshipping Him all the time by his relentless service and devotion to his parents. When the Lord himself visited Pundalika, he was massaging the feet of his father and was requested to sit on a brick there. The Lord obliged to the request and gave a boon to Pundalika, satisfied and pleased with his care towards his parents. The son was blessed by Lord for performing his dharmic duty to his parents. It is believed that serving the parents is the Divine Command to all Hindus. Lord Vishnu has pointed up the importance of this duty because the parents take His responsibility in guarding the children on earth and therefore considered as His representatives on this planet earth. He made it clear that serving our parents is equal to worshipping Him. In His discourse to sage Markandeya, Lord Vishnu has said –

"My best Bhaktas are those who worship his father as Lord of this universe, and his mother as the Holy River Ganga" – Narada Purana 1.5.53

Pundalika's story stands a proof to His words. The importance of loving the parents is explained by a mythological story involving Lord Ganesh and Lord Karthikeya. Their parents Lord Shiva and Goddess Parvathy explained to Karthikeya that parents precede anyone or anything else in the life of any person. They occupy the altar in a person's life and nothing is more important to him than the parents. Lord Ganesh realised this and won the divine fruit for his realisation on his devotion to parents. Another story is that of Sage Adhi Sankaracharya, who is thought by some section of Hindus as an Avthar of Lord Shiva, who diverted the river Purna for the benefit of his aged mother Aryamba.

Perhaps no other kavya or Purana has stories of sons showing exceptional devotion to their parents as that of the great epic Ramayana. Lord Ram himself is an excellent example of a dharmic person. He renounced his kingdom and went to forest for fourteen years when His father asked so. He forgave step-mother Kaikeyi, who was instrumental behind this saga, for her misdeeds. He was such a devoted son that he never asked any reason for his father's decision and He just obeyed his wish. In the same epic Ramayana, there is the pathetic story of a young man Shravankumar who carried his aged and blind parents in a kavadi whenever they are on move. The boy tended his parents with utmost devotion and care. He was the personification of a devoted son. As fate would have been it, he fell to the arrows of Dasarath, father of Lord Ram.

It was a mistake and Dasarath, a virtuous king, had no intention to harm the young boy. The entire Ramayana is hinged on the killing of Shravankumar.

It can be seen that Hinduism is replete with stories of devoted sons and it is a culture which practices what it preaches. Not to be left behind, Srimad Bagavatham, one of the 18 puranas narrates how Lord Krishna fulfilled his duties to His parents and teacher. Lord Krishna's biological parents, Vasudeva and Devaki, were incarcerated by His demonic maternal uncle Kamsa and were subjected to untold miseries. As a dutiful son, Lord fought with his uncle, killed him and liberated His parents from prison. Srimad Bhagavatham narrates how Lord Krishna paid respects to His teacher, guru, the sage Sandeepani. In the ashram of Sandeepani, Krishna created a sacred tank, Gomti Kund and filled it with water from all holy rivers by summoning them and thus obviating the need for the aged and infirm guru to travel to other holy places to take bath in holy rivers. After the completion of studies, it is custom that the students pay guru dhakshina, a sort of fees, to their guru. When asked about his wish, the guru asked Krishna to bring back his son who was lost to the ocean. Krishna went to Lord of death, Yama and brought back the departed son back to His guru. These stories explain that even God is bound to pay obeisance to His parents and teacher and He does that so willingly.

In the other epic Mahabharat, Duryodhana, the Kaurava king, was personified as a person of evil thoughts, full of disrespect, hatred and full of bile towards his elders and teachers, though they were aged, experienced and immensely more skilled than him. He was not known to have yielded to the wisdom of his parents and elders and always disobeyed their commands. It is this defiant and incompliant attitude towards his elders and teachers led to his downfall.[8] It is reiterated in Srimad Bhagavatam in verse 10.4.46. It says that all blessings which a person received by means of his prayers for longevity, beauty, fame and salvation will become naught when he ill treats a noble soul. Srimad Bhagavatm says in verse 1.9.12 that a man who vigorously follows the steps of the religious principles need not lose courage and not to be crestfallen when the circumstances are not favourable to him. The comportment and mien of Pandavas towards the same elders and gurus were distinctly in contrast to that of Kauravs. In spite of having been subjected to prejudice and innumerable hardships, Pandavas showed great reverence and deference to the parents of Kauravas and served them till they remained in the kingdom. Similarly in the battlefield, Arjuna refuses to fight when he is faced with his great grandfather and teachers on the opposite side. Bhagavat Gita in verse 2.4 says that he was unwilling to fight with his elders and teachers who are worthy of his worship. The scriptures, sastras and smritis prohibit a person to fight a war with his elders even if they attack him. Even if they behave harshly at sometimes, it is not justifiable to treat them in a similar way. Once again, this directive can be exemplified with the character of Prince Prahalad. He was tortured and was mercilessly ordered to be killed by his own cruel father. In spite of these, Prahalad was very humble and respectful to his father and was never abrasive in his behaviour with his father. According to Vedic pundits, devotion and deference to parents always gets a person closer to God.

Thus, it is believed in Hinduism that being in service of one's parents leads to great rewards and has stressed that such obeisance

---

8   Disrespect Leads to Downfall, H. H. Mahavishnu Goswami Amrtavani, available at: <https://www.mahavishnugoswami.com/gr/5048>, (last accessed on May 05, 2025).

is for his own good. On the other hand, neglecting them leads to bad karma. No amount of prayers will bear fruit for the person who has abandoned his parents. An individual, irrespective of his age, draws his economic, emotional and social support from his family. An elderly person largely manages to cope with the challenges and changes in income, health and social life with the help of his immediate family members to a large extent and others like friends and well wishers, to a lesser degree. The support from his family members is more dependent on culture based rather on development index of the society or country he lives in. Indian culture, more notably Hindu culture mandates to respect not only the elderly members of the family, but also to treat his parents and teachers in reverence. Hinduism made it mandatory the assimilation of elderly in its culture and set an example to the entire world how smooth the system works. The Disengagement Theory (Cummings and Henry) of the western civilization states the declining roles of the elderly persons as a prerequisite for the continuance of the society. This is in complete contrast with the Indian cultural belief and custom that elderly persons are an inalienable part of the family and society. These two differing cultural views are indicators of cultural relativity.

2.2. Filial and Elderly Care in Buddhism and Jainism

Both Buddhism and Jainism were established in ancient India. The founder of Buddhism, Gautama Buddha and the proponent of Jainism, Mahavir, are accepted as contemporaries though there is no evidence that they have ever met. Many historians believe that Buddha lived between c 563 BCE to 483 BCE and Mahavir was thought to have born little earlier. There are lot of similarities in both the religions and they share many common beliefs. Both preach sramana ascetic traditions and believe that it is possible to attain mukthi, liberation from birth cycle, through adherence to strict spiritual disciplines. There was widespread discontentment prevailing at that time with the Vedic Brahmanic traditions and rituals and both the religions showed immense disregard to these rituals. Both preached love, non-violence and sympathy as the path to salvation. Both the religions attained popularity and acceptance among many kings of that time and hence with their subjects. For example, the founder of Maurya empire, Chandragupta Maurya embraced Jainism and breathed his last by starving himself as per the Jain tradition in the state of Karnataka. His son Bimbisara was a benefactor and follower of Buddha. His son Ashoka, the known first emperor of Indian sub continent, was an avid follower of Buddhism and was reason behind for the spread of Buddhism in Southeast Asian countries. All the three major 'dharmic' religions existing during 6th century BCE viz. Hinduism, Buddhism and Jainism vied with each other to gain widespread acceptance and supremacy among kings and people during those ancient Indian period. This continued even during medieval period though the arena largely shifted to south India during that period. It was not uncommon among the kings to embrace another faith different from their initial religion and persecute the other religious followers under the influence of preachers of their new religion.

However, Buddhism and Jainism slowly waned in their popularity and Hinduism regained its original glory and the influence of former two were restricted to some regions in India at the end of medieval period. As noted earlier, all these shared many common beliefs such as conscientiousness, sathya, rebirth, salvation etc... though some of the concepts are interpreted in slightly divergent manners. Even within the same religion, the concepts are approached in moderately dissimilar ways according to the sects. Many followers of these three religions and along with Sikhism, which originated 15th century, do not consider these faiths as in opposition to each other. Even today, they are considered belonging to the same extended cultural family. All the Indian dharmic religions have laid great emphasis, inter alia, on the deference and devotion to elders, especially parents. There have been references to the importance and duty of children to take care of parents during their old age in the inscriptions of emperor Ashoka of Mauryan dynasty. The religious scripts and teachings had great influence on the maintenance of parents during ancient India. Due to these religious exertions, the status of elders was largely satisfactory in ancient India. It will be pertinent and befitting to go through some of the available homilies and sermons so as to understand the influence they had on the care taking of aged parents and elders during ancient times.

2.2.1. Filial and Elderly Care in Buddhism

Buddhism insisted and underscored the importance of parents in one's life. Parents are the founts of every one's life. It has been wisely stated that they are the sun and moon of one's family and the world.

It accentuated the need to take care of them at many instances. Buddha articulated that,

> *"Even if one should carry about ones mother on one shoulder and ones father on the other, and so doing should live a hundred years.... Moreover, if one should set them up as supreme rulers, having absolute rule over the wide earth abounding in the seven treasures – not even by this could one repay ones parents. And why! bhikkhus, parents do a lot for their children: they bring them up, provide them with food, introduce them to the world.*
>
> *Yet, bhikkhus, whoever encourages their faithless parents, and settles and establishes them in faith; or whoever encourages their immoral parents and settles and establishes them in morality, or whoever encourages their stingy parents, and settles and establishes them in generosity, or whoever encourages their foolish parents, and settles and establishes them in wisdom – such a person, in this way repays, more than repays, what is due to their parents."* [9] *– Anguttara Nikaya: 2. 32*

The earliest Buddhist resources such as Nikayas and Agamas inform us of the importance of filial piety. Buddhism expounded that being grateful is a positive response and a life without any gratitude is desolate and will rob the light out of existence. The children have to be grateful for the kindness, love and generosity that they have received from their parents. The children need not be

---

9   Russell Webb, *An Analysis of the Pali Canon* 439 (Buddhist Publication Society, 1975).

judgemental if the parents have erred. Buddha was of the opinion that the parents need to be honoured as Brahma, the eternal God. He advised his followers to show deference to the Brahma at home, who are none other than the parents. Thus he has placed the parents on the highest pedestal in the society. He asserted that the two people who cannot be paid back for all their good deeds to the children are mother and father

"Dvinnāham bhikkhave na suppatikāram vadāmi matucca pitucca" – Anguttara Nikaya: II

He further said that

"Sukhā matteyyatha loke, atho petteyyathā sukhā" – Dhammapada 332

Which means that, "Ministering to mother is a very pleasant thing and ministering to father is very pleasant thing in the world." Buddha said that the mother's milk that we drank is worth more than all the water in the oceans. A family which has good and kind hearted parents is greatly blessed and is considered as fortunate enough. Buddha himself was a model of a good son. He maintained his parents, during their old age, by earning alms to feed them. He exacted the children to repay the obligation to their parents by taking care of them when they are in need of it. Honouring the parents is the foremost of all good karmas as per Buddhist teachings. He further expounded that any unfortunate incidents of either patricide or matricide are the two most sinister karmas which will result in rebirth in hell. In the Ekottar agama, killers of parents are one among the eleven kinds of people who cannot reach the noble eightfold pathway. Such evil action result in two of the five gravest bad karmas. Persons who have indulged in matricide and patricide are not to be admitted into the Buddhist order, as per Pali vinaya. Such persons should be expelled from the order, if they had been already admitted. It has been stated that all moral teachings stem out of filial piety which is the root cause of all moral rectitude. Using a sacrificial terminology which was widely practiced during his time, Buddha named three types of fires which should be honoured with care are parents, family members and religious men and not the sacrificial fire which he considered as a heretic practice. Parents who appear first in the list are called as root fires since they are the reason for the existence of children and this root should be shown due reverence, honour and respect. Buddhism extends the honour to be paid by the children to their ancestors who have passed away by means of offerings to them, feeding the famished spirits and transferring the merits of good deeds that are done in the name of the deceased. This is a part of ancestor worship as per Buddhist traditions.

Buddhism considers the obligations to the mother, to the father, to the Tathagata (the enlightened one) and to the Dharma teacher are tough to be fulfilled. Buddha explains, in the following verses, that those who honour their parents will find a place in Heaven.

> *"Mother and Father are like gods, they are our very first teachers, as they are kind to their children, They are worthy of offerings.*
>
> *Therefore the Wise will worship them, and respect them with gifts of clothes, food and drink; with a sleeping place, with massage, bathing, and washing.*
>
> *The Wise, because they look after, both their mothers and their fathers, will be praised right here and now,*

and later rejoice in Heaven" – Anguttara Nikaya: 3.31 Sabrahmakasutta[10]

The five reasons that parents are desirous of a child, as per Buddha, are

"Considering these five reasons, the wise wish for a child, thinking: supported he will support us, he will do his duties for us,

They support mother and father, remembering what they have done, they perform their duties for them, as was done for them in the past.

Listening to parents' advice, feeding those who supported him, not neglecting his heritage, endowed with faith and with virtue, that child is praised and respected" – Good children ; Anguttara Nikaya: 5.39 Puttasutta

Buddha denounces the ingrate and coarse child, who does not offer care and maintenance to the aged parents, is as an outcaste. He was categorical on this assertion in his discourse on outcastes.

"Yo mātaram vā pitaram vā jinnakam gata yobbanam pahusanto na bharati tam jaññā vasalo iti". – Wasala Sutta

(The meaning is that the one who does not maintain his parents, in spite of being of being wealthy, is an outcaste)

---

10 Buddhist Wisdom Verses – 26: Children, available at: <https://ancient-buddhist-texts.net/English-Texts/Buddhist-Wisdom-Verses/26-Children.htm> (last accessed on May 05, 2025).

Conversely, a person who looks after his parents is blessed, as Buddha has stated in his Blessing Discourse

"Mātā pitu upatthānam etam mangalam uttamam"
– Mangala Sutta[11]

Buddha has listed in Sigalovada Sutta of the Dighanikaya, the five duties of the children towards the parents.

1. Taking care of them with the four basic requirements – food & drinks, clothes, a roof over them, and medicine (Bhato vā no bharissati)
2. Feeding them, bathing them, massaging them and helping them in those chores which they are unable to do (Kiccam nesam karissati)
3. Maintain the family tradition, image and name (Kulawamsam thassati)
4. Behaving worthy of the parent's inheritance (Dāyajjam patipajjissati)
5. Performing meritorious duties in their names even after their death and transfer those merits to them (Atha ca pana petānam kālakatānam dakkhinam anupadassati).

Filial piety is a virtue that has been repeatedly emphasised in Buddhism. Children are required to take care of the elders, not as an imposed cultural duty but as a gratitude for all the love and care received earlier from them. The obligation has to be carried out without frustration and bitterness. Dhammapada, a collection of verses of teachings of Buddha says that life span, beauty, happiness and strength increases to the one who honours and pays homage

---

11 Why should we respect and support our parents – Bhikkhu T. Seelananda, available at: <https://www.jendhamuni.com/respect-support-parents> (last accessed on May 05, 2025).

to elders[12]. Filial piety releases a child from the debts he has incurred from his parents towards his birth, care and upbringing. It is a moral, ethical and meritorious deed required by the culture. It is a dharma practice which is essential to maintain social order. Buddha has said in Anguttanikaya that filial piety is one of the three praiseworthy duties. Even a monk is no exception to this filial duty. In spite of his worldly renunciations, he is obligated to attend them in times of their need as expounded in Vinaya. We can draw a parallel to this in Hindu saint Sankaracharya who lit fire to his mother's pyre amidst the objections of followers of Vedic traditions. Buddhist texts have narrated the story of Ghatikara, a potter and a follower of Buddhism, in Ghatikara Sutta of the Majjhimanikaya. He remained a bachelor for serving his aged blind parents in spite of his longing to become a bhikku. Here also, a parallel can be drawn to the story of Shravanakumar in the Hindu epic Mahabharath, who tended to his aged and blind parents. In the Ekottar agama, it has been elucidated that any offerings that are made to the parents is equal to that offerings that are made to bodhisattva[13].

2.2.2. Filial and Elderly Care in Jainism

As per Jain philosophy, there is no creator of the world or universe. It is considered eternal which does not have a beginning or end. Nor the followers of Jainism worship any God. A Tirthankara is followed and revered as a savior. He is a spiritual teacher of the righteous path who has attained liberation from birth cycles on their own. They became 'Jina', an ideal to be followed by whoever wants to

---

12 Respect to the Elders, *available at* <https://mettainaction.files.wordpress.com/2012/06/2010-02-mia_respect-to-the-elders-burma-update-feb-2010.pdf> (last accessed on May 05, 2025).

13 Guang Xing, "Filial Piety in Early Buddhism", *Journal of Buddhist Ethics* 88 – 112 (2005).

attain such spiritual enlightenment. The Jains worship his qualities to become a Jina[14].

Jainism also speaks highly of the reverence to be shown to elders, including the parents. It says that one cannot retain knowledge if he does not show honour and deference to the parents, teachers and religious books etc... Bowing down to monks and elders, having decent manners and listening to parents are some of the respects one shows in Jain culture. Having respect induces good thoughts, destroys ego and leads to kindness towards all living beings. Jainism asserts that anyone who is older than one person is considered as an elder to him. It is obligatory that he is to be addressed respectively and to be polite with him. Elders are to be listened with attention without any interruption. Jainism further says that anyone who is more knowledgeable is also to be considered as an elder. The teachers, preachers of religion and those who spread ethical values are also to be respected as elders. Age is not the guiding factor to be called an elder, but it is their knowledge that determines. Their higher spiritual level renders them eligible for honour and respect. Jainism expounds the moral duty of the children to take care the parents and other elders with love and affection till the end of their earthly life.

---

14 Arun Kumar Jain, *Faith and Philosophy of Jainism*, (Kalpaz Publications, Lucknow, 2009).

2.3. Filial and Elderly Care in Islam

A perfect understanding of attitude of Islam towards old age and taking care of elders will requisite a reasonable study of Islam's religious principles and values. Taking care of aged parents is all the more necessary in the light of current, cultural, psychological and ever changing socio-economic circumstances and needs. The transitions and transformations that the society is undergoing and the unsettling happenings around the globe make it mandatory to study the ancient concepts. In eastern hemisphere, interdependence takes precedence over individualism. The latter concept finds no place or unheard of in the joint family system. This interdependence, in the family system as followed in that part of the world, steer the acolytes of eastern religions to oblige the moral and ethical duty of showering love and deference towards their elders. Traditionalism springs from cultural values and convictions rather than from religious beliefs and dictates. But culture itself, more often, is an offshoot of religion. Being solicitous, in Islam, towards parents stems from tradition and religious edicts. Scriptures and spiritual texts have found to have placed elders on a high pedestal and advised the followers that the parents are worthy of praise and adulation.

Islam, like any other religion, stresses the importance of moral and ethical values that have to be maintained in the society for a peaceful existence. It also emphasises the role of elders in maintaining the equity, peace, righteousness, morality and ethics in the society. In the process, it accords great importance to take care of the elders who are the back bone of the society. The religion's stance on old age is largely based on religious beliefs, rules and practice. As in other many of the religions and cultures, family set up forms the bedrock of the society and is the basic unit of such a society. The family set up, as a building bloc, enables the assimilation of elderly relatives into the society. It assures catering to the needs of aged parents. Elderly people play the most indispensable role during the lifetime of a Muslim, right from cradle to grave. As in eastern culture, it is a common sight for the aged parents to live with their children as a part of an extended family which may include grandparents, aunts, cousins, nieces and nephews. As the head of the family, elderly occupy an exalted status and are greatly venerated within the family and society. They perform multiple roles such as arbitration of family disputes, providing advice and suggestions, imparting wisdom, handling a predicament, care taking of grandchildren etc...Elders can also be a source for reshaping conventional social culture in symphony with changing times. Elders help us to make informed decisions in every day walk of life. Being in the vicinity of them brings additional human capital and wisdom.

Quran has extensively dealt with the care that has to be endowed on parents in various verses and surahs. Allah has dictated that we should not show even the slightest repugnance towards parents[15]. The Muslims follow the dictates of Prophet who himself received the commands from the Allah, the supreme legislator for them, through angel Gabriel (Alihi-wa-Sallam). These commands were later compiled into Holy Quran by Prophet himself. The Sharia law which comprises the rules followed by Muslims is based on Quran – the sayings of Allah, Sunnah – sayings of Allah as quoted by prophet which are not included in Quran, Hadith – a narration of words and actions of Prophet, Fiqh – The theory comprising Islamic jurisprudence based on Quran and the traditions of Prophet, Ijma – consensus opinions of disciples of Prophet and Islamic scholars

---

15 Abad Ahmad, *Understanding Islam: Its Spirit and Values*, (HarperCollins, India, 2019).

on Islamic law, Qiyas – deductive analogy employed to apply a new injunction, Istihsan – the principles of legal thinking underlying scholarly interpretation, Istihab – fundamental Islamic principle of legal deduction , Urf – source of rulings for instances which are not mentioned in Quran and Sunnah. As said before, the religious and cultural value system of the Islamic society finds its origin in the Islamic religious teachings and Hadith. In the book of Al-adab al-mufrad , a topical book of Hadiths, seeking to perfect the manners of Muslims, Al-Ash'ari has reportedly said that

> *"Part of respect for God is to show respect to an old Muslim."*[16]

As the well known hackneyed phrase goes, charity begins at home. It is reverberated in the sayings of Ibn Arabi, the famous Andalusian Muslim scholar, mystic, poet, and philosopher, who said that the criteria of charity is satisfied and complete by supporting one's family. Such an act simultaneously sustains the family kinship also. Muslim religious teachings have established the necessity of elderly care and the Hadith says that those desirous of longer life and well being should kindly take care of his relatives. Both the Islamic society and religion exhorts its members to give primacy to the elders. It demands that the congregational prayers and public functions are to be led by an elderly person. Also, Prophet reportedly advised his followers to "Begin with elderly", according preference to them in public functions[17]. The parent-child relationship is next only to the husband – wife relationship in a family. The sacrifices

---

16 Caring for the Elderly, available at: <www.dar-alifta.org> (last accessed on May 06, 2025).

17 Harasankar Adhikari, *Elderly in Muslim Community*, (Countercurrents, Feb 26, 2019), *available at* <https://countercurrents.org/2019/02/elderly-in-muslim-community/> (last accessed on May 06, 2025).

made by the parents are well recognised by the religion and it stresses that they deserve obedience and gratefulness from their children. Often the parents have not had any paved high ways and would have strived hard to place food on the dining table for their children at the end of the day. A person needs to understand the difficulties the parents would have endured to bring them up. He needs to know his past to cope with the present and look for the future. The ultimate mandate regarding this is the Quranic verse wherein Allah has enjoined compliance towards one's parents along with His own worship.

> *"Be grateful to Me and both your parents" – Surah Luqmān 31:14*

> *"And your Lord has commanded that you shall not serve (any) but Him, and goodness to your parents" – Surah al-'Isrā', 17:23*

The Holy text Quran says that

> *"And your Lord has ordained that you shall worship none save Him and shall do your parents a good turn."*[18]

Here, the phrase good turn is interpreted as repaying the favours they made to the children. It means, paying obeisance, remaining obedient, being affable and warm to their feelings and sentiments, catering to their physiological and psychological requirements and praying to the Lord to have mercy on them and bless them. The Prophet has said that,

---

18 Dr. I. A. Arshed, "Parent-Child relationship in Islam", *available at* <https:// www.islam101.com/sociology/parchild.htm>, (last accessed on May 06, 2025).

"If either or both of them reach old age with you, say not to them (so much as) "Ugh" nor chide them, and speak to them a generous word. And make yourself submissively gentle to them with compassion, and say;

O my Lord! Have compassion on them, as they brought me up (when I was) little" – Quran, 17:23-24

Islam says that it is an ethical obligation both to an individual and to the community as a whole to treat the elders with reverence and take care of them. This attitude of deference to elders is the cultural, moral, ethical and religious norm. The Hadith says that

"He is not one of us who does not show mercy to our young ones, and esteem to our elderly"

"He who honours an old man for his old age – meaning during his old age – God will grant him one to honour him during his old age"

Allah has commanded the people to be kind to their aged parents and not to be shown disrespect. He further ordained that the children should not utter harsh words or berate them. They should be treated kindly and humbly. This best exemplifies the stance of Islam towards the serving of aged parents. By extension, it places an obligation on its followers to take care of other elders also. On the demise of the parents, the children have the burden of taking care of next of kin of their parents' viz. aunts, uncles.

The Prophet said that

"Those who do not show mercy to our young ones and do not realize the rights of our elders are not from us"
– Sunan Abu Dawud

If the children are not dutiful of them, they stand disgraced in the eyes of God. The Prophet had said that

> *"May he be disgraced! May he be disgraced! May he be disgraced, whose parents, one or both, attain old age during his lifetime, and he does not enter Jannah (by being dutiful to them)"*

Annoyance or humiliation or disobedience towards the parents leads to the indignation of God. Traditions from Prophet reveal that one of the greatest sins is to be disobedient to parents.

> *"Do not look at them with distaste. Do not raise your voice above theirs. When you walk with them do not precede them. When you go to a gathering, do not sit before they do. Never keep your hand above theirs (while giving them something)"*[19]

The Holy text says that whatever one spends should be spent on Allah, on his parents, his close relatives, on foundling children, impecunious people, and travellers who are in need of money in alien lands. It has been told that:

> *"Be good to your parents and if they are in need of something, procure it for them before they ask for it."*

It has been mentioned in Quran wherein Hazrzt Yahya (John the Baptist) has asked the Muslims to be kind towards to their parents and not to have a stern and insubordinate attitude towards them. It narrates how Hazrat Yousuf (Joseph) took care of his old and infirm parents. He invited them from their home at a far off place and did not have any qualms to seat them, the poor parents,

---

19 A Divine Perspective on Rights, "Right of the Older One", *available at* <https:// www.al-islam.org/greater-sins-volume-1> (last accessed on May 06, 2025).

on a high platform in his ministry. Hazrat Isa (Jesus) has told his followers that Lord has made him considerate towards his mother and he was not defiant or harsh on her. There is an anecdote depicted in Quran in which Prophet has reportedly said that one cannot pay and recompensate for what his mother did to him for his growing up[20]. In Islam, the mother should be shown gratification three times to that of a father, as per the tradition of the Prophet since she underwent through more difficulties in giving birth and rearing up the child. He further added that

> *"If the service to a mother equals the quantity of the particles of sand in the desert and the drops of rain on earth, it (this service) will not repay for a single day that she kept you in her womb" – Mustadrak – ul-Wasa'il*

Be that as it may, the above are the very few of the millions of reasons for a son needs to be devoted and thankful to her. And the Hadith asserts that

> *"Paradise lies under the feet of the mother",*

which means that serving the mother leads the children to the Paradise. Allah has said that,

> *"We have enjoined man concerning his parents: His mother carried him through weakness upon weakness, and his weaning takes two years. Give thanks to Me and to your parents. To Me is the return" – Quran 31:14 Qara'i*

---

20 Kristine J. Ajrouch, "Caring for Aging Muslim Families: A Needs Assessment", *Institute for Social Policy and Understanding, New York*, (2016).

The importance of mother is amplified by another tradition which commands to show similar kind of proclivity to the close relatives on her side and as well to her friends. A service to parents leads to the blessings of Lord and He stands by us and saves us during times of hardships. This can be best exemplified by an allegory which explains how three persons got entrapped in a cave during their journey on a rainy day. The stone that blocked the entrance of the cave would not give way when they tried to come out of the cave. They begged Allah to save them by narrating the good deeds they have done in past. The beneficent acts done by them included the service to their parents and on this, the stone gave way and thus they are saved. Islam enjoins its followers to care for the needs of not only their parents, but also all elders.

It is an Islamic belief that persons enter paradise through their care, devotion and deference to their parents. Islam says that teachers also have a very special place in the life of a Muslim. They impart us knowledge (Ilm) which endears us to God and convert us as better human beings. Soul is said to be loftier than the physical body. In a similar manner, the teachers of humanity, the Spiritual fathers are placed on a higher pedestal than the biological parents. A disobedience to the spiritual father warrants a more severe punishment than a disobedience to a real parent. In a similar vein, the service and deference to a spiritual father is guerdoned thousand times more for a similar gesture to a biological parent.

Quranic Ayats state that

> *"And We have enjoined on man goodness to his parents" – Surah Al-Ankabūt 29:8*

"Be grateful to Me and both your parents..." – Surah Luqmān 31:14

It is to be noted from the above that Allah has mentioned together importance of gratefulness towards Himself and to the parents. Thankfulness to both Allah and parents are called Wajib.

The Holy Prophet (S) said: ".... to serve parents for a day and night is equal to a year of Jihad."

Another tradition from Holy Prophet says outlining the punishment for neglecting parents.

"Acquire your place in Heaven by serving your parents. If you are guilty of 'Āq' then make Hell your abode."

The Prophet said that being good to parents expiate the sins one has committed. The Holy Prophet has said

"do goodness to your father in order that your sins may be expiated".

The Holy Prophet has further stated,

"In the happiness of parents lies the happiness of Allah and in their dissatisfaction is Allah's dissatisfaction."

"Benevolence to parents is the greatest of the religious obligations"

He has elevated the status of children who look after their parents by stating that

"A person who is good to his parents will be just a grade below the prophets in Heaven. And the disobedience to parents will be only a grade higher than the Fir'ons (Pharaoh, the Egyptian dictator) in Hell" – Mustadrak ul-Wasa'il

It has been tradition in Islam that

"Secret charity cools down Divine anger while goodness to parents and benevolence to relatives, prolongs life" – Bihār al-Anwār

Another tradition says that,

"Benevolence to parents and secret charity ward off poverty and both (these deeds) prolong life. Seventy types of death are kept away" – Bihār al-Anwār

The Muslim scholar Hazrat Imam Rid'a said that munificence to parents is righteous (Uyūn al-Akhbar ar-Rid'a). In the event of the death of parents, the children have to perform good deeds on their behalf. Allah, on pleased with this, will rain His grace and kindness on them. Being kind to parents secures double awards. The first one is for the deed itself and the second one for the indulgence towards them. It is mandated in Quran that a person should not harm his parents, nor he should allow anybody else to harm them. Hazrat Imam Naqi has reportedly stated that,

"The displeasing of parents causes decrease in sustenance and degradation (also follows)"

There was an anecdote of an opulent person from Madinah who was negligent of his duty towards his parents nor used his affluence for their well being. He became poor as a punishment for his insolence and dereliction of his filial duty. The prophet has observed that "the misdeeds of the person has cost his place in heaven and fire of hell is awaiting him". The Muslim scholar Ja'far as-Sadiq said that those who behave uprightly to relatives and considerate towards parents will not go through difficult chapter in their life and will be prosperous. And they will leave this world peacefully. The Prophet has said that

"Those who assure me that they will be benevolent to parents and do good to the relatives, I will give them excess of wealth and a long life and assure them of being close among our group" – Mustadrak ul-Wasa'il

As said earlier, injunctions from Quran and Sunnah inform us that the parents need to be maintained and treated with reverence, kindness and equity. Maintenance by a person is defined as expenditure occurred towards the sustenance of his dependents and others for whom the person is legally responsible[21]. It includes food, clothing and roof over his head. Maintenance should be beneficial and good for the dependents and the money spent is from the earning and the property of the maintainer. Allah has said that

".... And extend to them a wing of humbleness out of compassion, and say: My Lord, bestow Your grace upon them, as they raised me and cherished me when I was little..." – Quran, 17: 23-25

In another verse, He further said that

".... keep their company in this world's life with kindness..." – Quran, 31: 14-15

The Prophet has warned the children who are insolent towards the parents since it is regarded as one of the gravest sins. The edict is also applicable to the children of those parents who do not follow the faith of Islam. It has been repeatedly mentioned in Quran at many instances on this.

"...You shall not serve any but Allah and (you shall do) good to (your) parents – Quran, 2: 83

---

21 Dinshaw Fardunji Mulla, Principles of Mahomedan Law 248 (Lexis Nexis, 23rd edn., 2021).

*... serve Allah and do not associate anything with Him
and be good to the parents – Quran, 4: 36*

*...you do not associate anything with Him and show
kindness to your parents" – Quran, 6: 151... 12*

Prophet has said that while spending money, a person should give priority to his parents till the standard of living of the parents, as far as food, clothing and shelter are concerned, is at par with the son. The maintenance in Muslim law means food, clothing and housing expenditures and is called as 'nafaka'. Quran has categorically asserted that

*"And give to the near of kin his due and (to) the needy
and the wayfarer and do not squander wastefully" –
Quran, 17: 26*

And Prophet has said that parents have a right to spend a portion of their children's wealth. Prophet has issued an injunction to a follower that,

"You and your wealth belong to your father".

In another instance He said that

*"Your children are among the best of your earnings,
so eat from your wealth"*

The children are goaded to support, from their earnings, their penurious parents who do not have any means by themselves. And this consideration towards parents hinges on an assorted list of conditions and exceptions such as the faculty of the children to do so and the circumstances.

It is not a requirement that parents must be incapable of doing any labour for the children to maintain them. Even if the son is not prosperous but is of sufficient earning capacity and is employed, he is bound to take care of the parents adequately. If the parents have many children, the son who is closest to them is obliged to maintain them irrespective of the circumstance whether he inherits the property or not. The obligation of maintaining the parents is shared equally among the children if they belong to the same social stature[22]. Under Muslim law, every person is obligated to take care of his dependents. As long as the dependents are in a precarious situation of not able to maintain themselves by their own earning, a son is made liable to take care of his parents, a husband has to take care of his wife, a father is duty bound to take care of his minor and major children. Both indigent parents, whether they are capable of earning or not, are to be taken care of by both the son and daughter coequally. When the children cannot offer them separate maintenance, the parents are entitled to live with them. There is a divergent view who has to be accorded priority when a son is capable of taking care of only one parent. While the Hanafi law bestows the precedence to the mother, Shia law dictates that care has to be divided between the destitute parents. A person of sufficient means has to maintain his penurious relatives who fall within the prohibited degrees, in commensurate with the share they are likely to be bequeathed. Children are not required to take care of relations by affinity. Another Islamic tradition states that both the impecunious maternal and paternal grandparents are also liable to be maintained by the son. If for any reason, the son, grandson, daughter and wife are unable to maintain the aged parents and grandparents due to infirmity, or being a minor or

---

22 Kharofa, *Ala'eddin, Islamic family law : a comparative study with other religions* 54 (Petaling Jaya, Selangor Darul Ehsan : International Law Book Services, Golden Books Centre, 2004).

being unmarried etc.. the onus of taking care of them falls on that person who is deemed to do so.

Hospitals, assisted care, old age homes have become the staple for the older generation throughout the world. The requirements of elders are varied. They require enough economic resources to meet their living needs, access to reasonable health care, integration with the community and society, to be in communication with their peers and relatives and lastly, but not the least, to be treated affectionately. Another major challenge faced by the elders is the social isolation. The children are put in a difficult situation wherein they are engulfed in shame when they are not able to take care of their parents during their decrepitude due to many constraints. Some children are filled with enormous contrite for their inability to take care of the parents. Muslim scholars are of the view that if the family situations do not permit to take personal care of their parents, hired help will be the alternate solution. Care must be taken that these hired help should not become a reason for the further slump in the health of the elders. This is a common occurrence in old age homes wherein we have come across instances of elders have been bullied, mistreated and abused. Endowments can be set up to assist persons who are willing to take up the care of elders within or outside the community. Well trained individuals can be provided employment for the service of elders at their homes itself. The expenses involved in addressing the wants and needs of elders is another stumbling block and for some people it may even be impractical. In some instances, they are considered as mere sink holes for the hard earned money.

Unlike in the western world, grandparents can be part of the nuclear family in Islam and the eastern part of the globe. However, the younger generation is often depicted as having radical views that are different from elderly people regarding family, religion, culture, custom and tradition. Their differing life styles, often in contradiction with each other, stands as a wall that is in the way. The aged people are often maltreated and are Cinderellas of the modern society in not getting the due and deserved attention. The difference lies in the fact that they may never get the fairy tale ending. Generational differences with their young children lead the elders to spend more time in the company of peers. For elders who had to migrate to new places for various reasons, threat of loneliness and isolation looms large. It is regret in a life full of them. Sometimes it may not be because of dearth of family connections but that of community. The changed life styles, different customs of the land and communication barriers make it tough to socialize beyond the family. Technology is found to be a divider between elders and young in the sphere of attitude, values and behaviour. Technology, at times, is conceived to devalue the experience and wisdom of elders. Lack of connectedness between different generations and communication barriers are other arenas that have to be addressed.

Meaningful interactions that are done in earnest lead to significant social relationships. This further will lead to an arena of well being. Foundering family relationships due to the forsaken duties will affect the processes of society and nation building. We are born with a tradition, custom, religion and culture and are often find ourselves fighting and rebelling against them. Perhaps, it might not be a bad idea to slip back into where we originated or came from. Life does not hand out another mulligan. We have to play our best the first time itself. Nor we get a second bite at the apple. Accordant, warm and affectionate relationships between the parents and children will fetch peace and serenity in the family which in turn will lead to a tranquil society and country.

Thus, Islam has taken a strong stand on the aspect of care towards elders. This can be seen throughout the Holy Quran and Sunnah. It is very lucid that children have been sufficiently advised to maintain their parents and other elders showing devotion and deference and be blessed for their care to them.

2.4. Filial and Elderly Care in Christianity

Christianity is followed by the most number of, nearly two billion, people in this world and is more spread geographically than any other religion. It stems from the life and teachings of Jesus. He is the central figure and essential character of the religion. It is suggested that one of the and the best possible ways to understand Christianity is to understand the earliest documents like four Gospels as well as the letters that are constituents of New Testament. It is a compilation of what Jesus taught, as remembered by earlier believers of the faith which are as felt and experienced by St Paul, St Matthew, St Luke etc... As in other major religions, there are numerous interpretations, different theologies and methods of worship and vastly divergent views on polity and governance of the community. It is said that Christianity is more than a system of faith and religious belief. Since the days of its foundation by Jesus, it has established a culture, developed religious practices, formed ideas and following different ways of life. Hence it may be said that it is a living tradition of faith and culture. In Christianity, true love is said to be sacrificial as demonstrated by Jesus by dying on cross for the sake of the people who loved and followed him. In a similar way, parents and children are required to make sacrifices for each other. A family set up is emphasized by the religion from which the children will learn about love, companionship, forgiveness, sacrifice selflessness etc. and such family set up forms the core of a community.

The relationship between elders including parents and children is reciprocal in nature. The elders while trying to be good care takers impart their hard gained wisdom to the child. Bible has given equal importance to the role of parents in nurturing and upbringing of their children. It is as important as taking care of the parents and elders by the children. Parents are required to provide to the needs of the children. And that includes spiritual needs also. The relationship between a person and God is a metaphor for the relationship between a parent and the child. The generosity of God as a parent is explained by Jesus as in,

> *"If ye then, being evil, know how to give good gifts unto your children, how much more shall your Father which is in heaven give good things to them that ask him?" –Matthew 7.11*

The nature of elders-children relationship is largely determined by the tradition as well as culture. In the western individualistic culture, the children are given more leeway to express their views and they are often an active participant in decision making process, especially which concerns the relationship between them and elders. In Eastern culture, children are often expected to toe the lines of parents' decisions and have limited freedom to express their views. The life style of a child of the eastern culture is strictly regimented under the watchful eyes of elders with an emphasis on discipline. It is imperative that traditional and cultural contexts have to be taken into account before evaluating whether parenting method is normative or not. The attitude of the children under a similar upbringing in a European or white American family and an African or Asian American family is vastly different. Children brought up under an overbearing and high handed atmosphere in White American family are found to be with negative outcome while a similar paternity behavior results in positive outcome in an Asian American family[23]. Culture plays the important role for these different attitudes. The cultural values placed on the deference

---

23 The Parent-Child Relationship – Chapter 4 from "Christianity and Developmental Psychopathology: Foundations and Approaches" Winston Seegobin, George Fox University, wseegobin@georgefox.edu.

and submission of the children of the eastern culture to the rigid and inflexible parenting style, honouring of family tradition, trust and confidence on the wisdom of elders result in the positive outcome in the mindset of the children. These children were found to be more confident, self assured and positive. In eastern culture, maintenance of family honor and harmony are greatly emphasized and are achieved by complying with the demands and wishes of the parents. Children are reckoned to show respect and honor to the elders and parents and they are demanded to obey the parents throughout their life time. It is a collectivistic culture where filial duties govern the children. It is a norm that the children have to take care of their elders and parents during their dotage and are expected to make considerable sacrifices, if need arises, in their own life. Following cultural values, traditions, norms and social rules are transmitted from generation to generation. In the individualistic western culture, children involve in the discussion on the needs of the parents and have a greater say in the outcome of it. Great sacrifices are not expected from the children as in the eastern world.

As in other traditions and culture, Christian traditions emphasize the importance of supporting children and elderly parents. As in other major religions of the world, parents and elderly community is venerated to a great extent in the Holy Bible. The scripture, the Bible, which every true Christian follows, points at many instances the moral and ethical obligation of children towards their parents. Such care is one of the Ten Commandments to be followed by every Christian. Early church has taken action to arrange for the care of needy people. St James, the Lord's brother, said that

> *"Religion that is pure and undefiled before God the*
> *Father is this: to visit orphans and widows in their*

affliction and to keep oneself unstained from the world" – James 1:27

The Christian religion urges its members to treat the parents with utmost honour and respect and goads them to be honest and obedient to them. At the same time, it commands the parents also their responsibilities since children are considered as a gift from God.

"Children, obey your parents...Parents, do not exasperate your children; instead, bring them up in the instruction of the Lord" – Ephesians 6:1-4

Bible at many places has prevailed upon the children to show reverence to the parents and the aged people[24]. Bible explains that serving and taking care of the elders including parents and grandparents is what that most is pleasing to God as in the following The New Testament text.

".... But if she has children or grandchildren, their first responsibility is to show godliness at home and repay their parents by taking care of them. This is something that pleases God very much." – 1 Timothy 5:3-4

When the children take care of their parents, they also obey the command of the Bible to honour the parents – Ephesians 6.2-3

Jesus has condemned the Pharisees who have chosen to neglect and forsake the parents and devised a way not to spend money on taking care of their parents by exploiting a loophole provision in the laws. They were too immersed in themselves and in their

---

24 Caring for Elderly Parents, available at: <https://www.openbible.info/topics/caring_for_elderly_parents> (last accessed on May 07, 2025).

selfishness to see the plight of the elders. Pharisees were a section of people who believed in resurrection. But they followed legal traditions of the fathers, and not that of Bible. A person is allowed to set a 'trust' offering to the church to circumvent the obligation of maintenance of parents, while simultaneously claim interest on their money. Jesus severely reprehends this act as it goes against the fifth commandment. *Jesus further censures them that apart from denying God's word, they are showing irreverence to their parents.*

> *"You have a fine way of setting aside the commands of God in order to observe your own traditions!" – Mark 7.9*

> *"Thus you nullify the word of God by your tradition that you have handed down. And you do many things like that." – Mark 7.13*

Jesus does not spare anyone who is impudent to his parents with a harsh curse.

> *"But you say, 'If a man tells his father or his mother, "Whatever you would have gained from me is Corban"' (that is, given to God)— then you no longer permit him to do anything for his father or mother, thus making void the word of God by your tradition that you have handed down. And many such things you do." – Mark 7:11-13*

> *"The eye that mocks a father and scorns to obey a mother will be picked out by the ravens of the valley and eaten by the vultures." – Proverbs 30:17*

> *"For God commanded, 'Honour your father and your mother,' and 'whoever reviles father or mother must surely die" – Matthew 15:4*

"Cursed be anyone who dishonours his father or his mother. And all the people shall say, 'Amen."

"Vengeance is mine, I will repay, says the Lord". – Deuteronomy 27:16

"For anyone who curses his father or his mother shall surely be put to death; he has cursed his father or his mother; his blood is upon him." – Leviticus 20:9

"But understand this, that in the last days there will come times of difficulty. For people will be lovers of self, lovers of money, proud, arrogant, abusive, disobedient to their parents, ungrateful, unholy.." – 2 Timothy 3:1-2

"If one curses his father or his mother, his lamp will be put out in utter darkness." – proverbs 20:20

It can be seen that as far as the filial piety is concerned, Christianity places the obligation on the children in alterations between offers of carrots and perils of stick. Bible places the children who do not obey their parents in the company of most horrible people.

"Slanderers, haters of God, insolent, haughty, boastful, inventors of evil, disobedient to parents" – Romans 1:30

"Whoever robs his father or his mother and says, "That is no transgression," is a companion to a man who destroys." – Proverbs 28:24

Christians are coaxed to take care of penurious relatives also, apart from maintenance of parents.

"Honor widows who are truly widows." –
1 Timothy 5:3

"Do not rebuke an older man but encourage him as you would a father, younger men as brothers, older women as mothers, younger women as sisters, in all purity.." – 1 Timothy 5:1-12

Responsibility towards and care taking of elders is foremost important. The excerpt below, taken from Bible, explains the above obligation for every Christian.

"If anyone does not provide for his relatives, and especially for his immediate family, he has denied the faith and is worse than an unbeliever" – 1 Timothy 5:8

The Apostle Paul was concerned with the care that was found wanting for destitute. He took to slamming the indolent attitude towards the needy. In the above verse, the Christians are told that such person is dissenting from the faith and teachings of God. And he is more abominable than non-believers of the faith. Paul ties the person's faith to the maintenance of needy people in their own house. It is said that such a disregarding conduct is shameful[25]. The Bible requires its followers to honour the elderly people.

"You shall stand up before the grey head and honour the face of an old man, and you shall fear your God: I am the Lord." – Leviticus 19:32

---

25 Elderly Care, "What the Bible Says about caring for parents" available at: <https://calvaryhomes.org/newsroom/what-the-bible-says-about-taking-care-of-elderly-parents> (last accessed on May 07, 2025).

"The glory of young men is their strength, but the splendour of old men is their grey hair" – Proverbs 20:29

"Gray hair is a crown of glory; it is gained in a righteous life." – Proverbs 16:31

"Wisdom is with the aged, and understanding in length of days." – Job 12:12

The fifth commandment behests the followers to honour both the parents. It follows with an assurance that the days of such adherents will be long.

"Honour your father and your mother, so that you may live long in the land the Lord your God is giving you" – Exodus 20:12

In this promise of living long – when or where – whether in this world or in eternity has not been mentioned. The verse denotes the positive consequence of honouring mother and father. Further, Jesus urges the people to follow the advice of their parents.

"Hear, my son, your father's instruction, and forsake not your mother's teaching, for they are a graceful garland for your head and pendants for your neck" – Proverbs 1:8-9

"My son, keep your father's commandment, and forsake not your mother's teaching. Bind them on your heart always; tie them around your neck. When you walk, they will lead you; when you lie down, they will watch over you; and when you awake, they will talk with you. For the commandment is a lamp and the teaching a light, and the reproofs of discipline are the way of life.." – Proverbs 6:20-23

"A wise son hears his father's instruction, but a scoffer does not listen to rebuke" – Proverbs 13:1

"Hear, O sons, a father's instruction, and be attentive, that you may gain insight, for I give you good precepts; do not forsake my teaching. When I was a son with my father, tender, the only one in the sight of my mother" – Proverbs 4:1-3

The children should not take pride in their duty of taking care of the parents or it should not get in the way of such care.

"In the same way, you who are younger, be subject to the elders. All of you clothe yourselves with humility toward one another, because God resists the proud but gives grace to the humble" – Peter 5:5

Peter has noticed how self-pride destroys the character of a person, or family, or institution and forewarns the children not to be get trapped by such a vice. Humbleness is the virtue that has to be strictly adhered to while serving the needy and a vainglorious attitude leads to ruin. When it comes to taking care of parents, the Bible elucidates in no uncertain terms the importance of it.

"Let your father and mother be glad; let her who bore you rejoice" – Proverbs 23:25

"Listen to your father who gave you life, and do not despise your mother when she is old" – Proverbs 23:22

"Every person must respect his mother and his father" – Leviticus 19:3

"God your Lord you shall respect, Him you shall serve" – Deuteronomy 10:20

The Torah says that one must show the same respect to the parents as he shows to God

> *"Children, obey your parents in everything, for this pleases the Lord" – Colossians 3:20*

> *"Children, obey your parents in the Lord, for this is right" – Ephesians 6:1*

> *"For Moses said, 'Honour your father and mother" – Mark 7.10*

> *"Every one of you shall revere his mother and his father, and you shall keep my Sabbaths: I am the Lord your God." – Leviticus 19:3*

> *"Do not cast me off in the time of old age; forsake me not when my strength is spent." – Psalm 71:9*

The Bible does not mention any specific instruction on the way or modalities of the elders are to be cared for. But there are enough commands by Jesus and his apostles in the scriptures and texts to take care of elders, parents and destitute. It is to be taken for granted that they are to be maintained in a serene atmosphere and made to spend the last part of their life in peace. Jesus adjures that

> *"Honour your father and mother, and, you shall love your neighbour as yourself." – Matthew 19:19*

> *"One way of honouring your parents is to love them as you love yourself."*

Jesus himself stood as an example of taking care of his mother during her old age. Even while going through enormous sufferings, for the sake of people, on the cross, he followed Paul's advice. His attentions were on his mother Mary, who is presumed to be a widow. As the firstborn son of the family whose primary duty is to look after the aged parents, he says to his mother,

"Woman, behold your son,"

and commands one of his disciples to take care of Mary,

"Behold your mother" – John 19:26–27

Jesus has seen to that she was not orphaned. Bible has mentioned a few other instances of how some of the biblical characters ensured that their elders are taken care of[26].

Joseph arranged for his aged father Jacob, who was living at a far off place, to move and live with him. Jacob was provided with food, clothes and shelter. All his needs were well taken care of by his son Joseph – Genesis 45:9-11; 47:11, 12.

Ruth moved to the house of her mother-in-law in another country and taken good care of the aged woman by working tirelessly – Ruth 1:16;2:2, 17, 18, 23.

Bible says that we should not be selfish and should care enough for others also. And that includes parents also[27].

"Do nothing from selfish ambition or conceit, but in humility count others"

"More significant than yourselves. Let each of you look not only to his own interests, but also the interests of others" – Philippians 2:3–4

---

26 Jehovah's Witnesses, "What does the Bible say about Caregiving for Elderly Parents"? available at <https://www.jw.org/en/bible-teachings/questions/elderly-caregiver-help/> (last accessed on May 07, 2025).

27 Pastor John, "Retirement Homes and Caring for Aging Parents" *available at* <https://www.desiringgod.org/interviews/retirement-homes-and-caring-for-aging-parents> (last accessed on May 07, 2025).

Apostle Paul urges the people to show Godliness. Maintenance of aged parents is a Godly act. It should be done as a duty and not to be assumed as a service to the society. Paul further exhorts to make some repayment to the parents. That is, it is the time to repay what parents did to the children. The children should have a sense of gratitude and obligation for all the care he received from his parents. And serve them when they are in need of it. Every parent would not have reached for the brass ring. Life is not meant to be like that. Everybody would not have had a three point landing. And they would not have been ideal parents a child wish to be. That could not be a justifying reason to neglect them during their old age. Irrespective of the fact whether the children had ideal care or not, it is the obligation of the child to maintain aged parents. Paul further stresses that serving the parents is a pleasing sight to God. Taking care of parents is a good fortune bestowed on us by God to show our love to Him. It is the God's call to look after the aged parents and is equal to serving and glorifying Him. It has been mentioned in Bible that

> *"Bear one another's burdens, and so fulfil the law of Christ." – Galatians 6:2–5*

It would be inapt to neglect the obligation of maintenance of parents due to the sheer exertion it may cause at times. They are the precious moments one spends with his parents which he will treasure after they pass into oblivion. Taking care of aged parents during the final leg of their life may pose many daunting obstacles that have to be overcome with empathy, love, sensitivity and poise. As new and challenging as to the children, parents are also encountering the issues for the first time as they walk through the most difficult phase of their life. Life is after all an uncharted territory, full of mysteries and challenges which have to be met as they come along. The issues the children may face are manifolds, the foremost being emotive. Coupled to this are financial and practical issues that prop up intermittently.

For many, life is not filled with equity. The life in this world is unfair is a factually correct statement. While some people are favoured by God to grow old with grace and pass away peacefully without any regrets, others are not accorded the same privilege. After all, life does not end wrapped up in a little bow for everybody. Many have to drudge even during their dotage and let the life slip away from them. The most difficult part of the life is when one faces life-ending diseases with hardly any one to support financially and morally. This can be seen as totally unjust and unfair. One may be rendered helpless in the face of destiny. But man has no other option except to accept it and grind our way through the life.

It will be misery to witness one's father reduced to a frail, fragile, frangible and crumbling skeleton figure, who once might have been a towering figure during his hey days, due to ill health. It will be miserable to watch him barely able to walk across his room, reduced from a pillar of strength, vanquished and battered by old age and diseases. It will be poignant moments of life time to watch the person who taught his children how to navigate the warrens of life, who imparted wisdom, who instilled courage to face hardships and who edified them to follow morality, slowly wither away. The emotional repercussions in those situations can be overwhelming. However, the Bible insists that during such crisis, it is important to remind ourselves the sufferings of Jesus

> *"But he was wounded for our transgressions, he was crushed for our iniquities; upon him was the chastisement that brought us peace, and with his stripes we are healed." – Isaiah 53:5*

In the midst of such horrendous experiences, the only silver lining is that the children have the opportunity of receiving the blessings of the parents by taking care of them and need not to live with regret later. The reminiscing happy moments one spends in serving the ailing aged parents will be etched in memory for ever.

The Christianity has clearly delineated the responsibility of maintaining the aged parents and the elderly relatives to the members of the immediate family. The church is already burdened with other issues. For all the requirements of elderly such as financial support, food, medicines and visit to hospital, the family is the front line of defence. Of course, the church steps in, when the elderly is an orphan, to take care of him or in other occasions when the family is unable to meet the hardships. If there is no one to take care of an elderly destitute, it places the onus on the church. Christians are urged to cater to the needs such as food, shelter, roof, pastoral care and social activities for such indigent elders through the institutions of church[28].

> *"The Church should care for any widow who has no one else to care for her." – 1 Timothy 5:3-4*
>
> *"If any believing woman has relatives who are widows, let her care for them. Let the church not be burdened, so that it may care for those who are really widows." – 1 Timothy 5:16*

The parents have not run out of children, but will they run out of care takers among them? Only time will answer it. We cannot let the elders to seek comfort in the arms of agony and solace in loneliness. Before the parents call it a day and bid adieu, the children

---

28 Elderly care – BBC *available at* <https://www.bbc.co.uk/bitesize/guides/ zj8qn39/revision/3 – Family life> (last accessed on May 07, 2025).

have to make sure that they start their final one way journey in peace. Every living person starts ageing from the moment he is born. As definitely as he ages, he too has to experience death. Birth and death are two distinct but conjoined events over which we don't have any leverage. But one can make the life of a parent filled with joy, contentment and tranquilness. We pray God that we may be blessed with the opportunity and facilities to serve our parents when they are in need of it. Let us be blessed with the wisdom needed to face the challenges in those duties. Let us be blessed to do what is most pleasing to Him. The care taker often has to make extraordinary sacrifices while looking after his aged parents and face numerous issues. The life style of the care taker and his family gets altered in various ways. The entire care taking family puts their life on hold to maintain the parents. Everything in their life revolves around their parents. While in a joint family there would be someone else to share the responsibility, the same luxury is not available in a nuclear family. The aged persons would require the same care and attention as a baby-toddler would. In the later case, the attention needed gets slowly come down as the baby grows while in the parents' case, the care required keeps multiplying as the days move on. It is common that the family will be consumed by various emotions like compassion, love, frustration, anger and guilt. Sometimes they will be stubborn and the children may feel that it is an otiose undertaking to make them to see the reason. Being in a lather over that does not make it right to reduce them to status and plight of a nonperson by our neglect. Patience is the key word while taking care of aged parents, especially if the parents are little unreasonable.

Historical Perspective

CHAPTER – 3

Filial and Elderly Care in India During Various Periods of History

Introduction

A man is a successor and descendent of a 'parampara'. The one option available to him to view, peruse, evaluate, assimilate, absorb and acquire the traditional values and mores of the culture is by viewing, being perched on the shoulders of the his elders through which he can uncover more knowledge by himself and adding to the already existing ones. The other option is to kneel at the feet of the ancestors to acquire the wisdom from them every moment, analysing the newly gained knowledge over the already inherited knowledge and apply them to the continuous changes that is occurring around them.[1] Obeisance to elders is a part of 'parampara. The tone of obeisance to elders is also an indication of the past. It may possibly show how the culture may progress in the coming days. This might cause an indelible impression on the personal as well as collective behaviour of the society. Indian culture is known to be flexible and never hesitated to have a fresh and open approach towards the demands of the present and has adopted itself to changing scenarios. And it did so without giving up its basic moral structure. In its travel on the

---

1   Metaphors of Reverence: A Tale of Two Civilisational Gestures, available at: <https://www.vifindia.org/article/2021/september/16/metaphors-of-reverence-a-tale-of-two-civilisational-gestures> (last accessed on May 15, 2025).

change of surface of Mobius strip, it may attain a new status in the future, as it has experienced many times in the past. But it keeps the traditions and culture refreshingly alive with more vitality since it has not forgotten to respect and honour their ancestors. And its culture never intends to forget its past also. Change and continuity are not viewed as binaries in such a culture; rather they are complementary to each other. The care and respect given to elders during various periods of Indian history are discussed in this part.

3.1. Filial and Elderly Care in India during Ancient Period

There are widespread disagreements among historiographers about the time line of ancient Indian civilisation. They are vertically divided according to the ideology they are adhered to. It is sad that historical impartiality is hardly given its due respect. Often, people are advised to know about the historian before reading the history he has written. Every history book is filled with bias and prejudice in line with the ideals of that of person who has penned it. This is especially true when the evidences available are very scant, diverse and contradictory and insufficient to deduce a reasonable and fair conclusion. For present purposes, the term ancient India refer to a period from the early 3rd millennium BCE when a literate culture is said to have begun to the end of the golden period of Indian history, the Gupta empire, during the early years of 6 the century, i.e. 500 CE. However there are other reports of a Saraswathi civilisation, along the banks of the vanished river, around 8000-10,000 years ago.

"Timeline of Indian history

2800 BCE: the beginning of Indus Valley civilization

1700 BCE: the end of Indus Valley civilization

500 BCE: birth of two religions, Buddhism and Jainism

327 BCE: Alexander's victory over Sind region and he conquers the Indus Valley; this leads to king Chandragupta Maurya of Maghada conquering the Indus Valley from Alexander's successor (304 BCE)

322 BCE Mauryan dynasty begins

269 BCE: Ashoka becomes the new Mauryan emperor

232 BCE: Demise of Ashoka and starting of decline of Mauryan Empire

150 CE: the Scythians (Saka) regime begins in northwest India

150 CE: the rise of Kushana Empire in northwest India

300 CE: The Gupta Empire begins

500 CE: the starting of decline of Gupta Empire"

The administration of justice during ancient India is available only from Mauryan dynasty[2]

3.1.1. Mauryan Dynasty

The Mauryan dynasty established by Chandragupta was the first historically recognised empire in India and it was s starting point for the future empires. However it continued for less than 150 years before its disintegration due to weak successors and policies. During it's hey days, the empire was spread over the entire north India. Chandragupta, Bindusara and Ashoka were the prominent kings of Mauryan dynasty. During Maurya period, all the three major religions of those days viz... Hinduism, Buddhism and Jainism vied with each other to gain prominence among the kings and their subjects. Chandragupta embraced Jainism during later stages of life and starved himself to death, as per Jain tradition, in Karnataka state. Bindusara was a follower and benefactor of Buddha. Ashoka converted to Buddhism, from Hinduism, after Kalinga war. He was instrumental in spreading Buddhism across India as well as China, Tibet, Sri Lanka and South East Asia. Till historian James Princep deciphered Brahmi inscriptions about Ashoka in1837, it was not

---

2   Timeline of the history of ancient India, *available at* <https://www.timemaps. com/civilizations/ancient-india/> (last accessed on May 07, 2025).

much known about him except for passing references. Since all the three religions venerated the elders and parents, it can be deuced that they might have enjoyed a pedestal status in the society. From the 'Arthsasthra', authored by the minister and benefactor of Chandragupta, it is possible to have a peek into the family structure during those ancient periods. It was not categorically mentioned what constitutes a family at those times, whether a joint family or extended family or nuclear family. However he has mentioned rights and duties of various members in the family. From his writings on inheritance, succession and partition rules on the wealth and properties of the family, it is possible to deduce that a typical family constituted a head of the family, usually the senior most male member, his wife, his sons, their wives, daughters and grand children[3]. The head of the family was the decision maker; but at times, the mother also participated in decision making process. It was said that Bindusara and Ashoka were used to feed about 60,000 Brahmins daily. Ashoka is famously known for his Dhamma, which is called 'dharma' in Sanskrit. These personal dharmic principles of Ashoka were deciphered from the inscriptions. These are different from 'Dhamma' of Buddhism as preached by Buddha. The salient points in Ashoka's dhamma persuaded his subjects not to kill human beings, not to destruct properties, to treat slaves and servants in a gentle way, to live in harmony with one another etc... People were asked to show deference to parents and elders and to honour teachers and mentors. People were instructed to take care of parents and elders[4]. He made sure to propagate his dhamma

---

3   Sun Tzu & Niccolo Machiavelli, *The Complete Strategy Collection: The Art of War, The Prince, The Book of Five Rings, On War and Arthashastra* 389 (CSA Publishing, 2022).

4   Ellis Roxburgh, *The Mauryan Empire of India* 287 (Cavendish Square Publishing, LLC, 2015).

principles across his kingdom and he himself took dhamma yatras to spread his principles and to influence his subjects. It has been mentioned that the kingdom took the destitute and widows under its wing and had taken proper care of them. Also, hospitals were maintained by the king for the aged people. It can be inferred from the little available references that parents and aged were well treated and had been taken proper care of.

3.1.2. Satavahana Dynasty

On the ruins of Maurya Empire and the successive rulers of Magadha, the dynasty of Satavahana was established with its centre at the present Paithan in Maharashtra. There are divergent views on their nativity. A more palatable view, from the inscriptions and numismatics evidences, is that they emanated from western part of India and extended and established themselves in the east coast and the name of Andhra dynasty got associated with them. Another inscription mentions that they (probably later Satavahanas) ruled from present Amaravathi in Andhra Pradesh. The founder of this dynasty, Simuka, wrested control of Magadha. His successors, particularly Satakarni I, expanded the kingdom in all the four directions particularly into the Godavari valley in south and Kalinga in the east. Satakarni I performed Asvamedha yagams and Rajasuya yagam, as a testimony of his military victories[5]. There was brief setback to their continuance of dominance over their military exploits due to Shaka clan kings and were confined to the eastern part of their earlier kingdom during the end of first century A.D to the beginning of 2nd century A.D. The fortunes of the dynasty were revived and the man of destiny this time was Gautamiputra

---

5   R. K. Sharma, II *The Ages of the Satavahanas: Great Ages of Indian History* 548 (Aryan Books International, Allahabad, 2002).

Satakarni, a house hold name in Andhra Pradesh (A.D. 106-130). By the dint of aggressive and efficient military campaigns, he subjugated many kingdoms and ruled over a vast empire covering an area from Konkan in the west to Berar in the east, Malwa and Saurastra in north to Krishna delta in the south. His successor Vashishthiputra Pulumayi (A.D. 130-154) seems to have ruled from their old capital Paithan on the banks of river Godavari. The dynasty seems to have come to an end in 220 A.D. [6] and the Rastrakuta dynasty was established on the decline of Satavahana Empire.

The people lived happily and were prosperous under the Satavahana rule. Agriculture and trade flourished. Many traits of Mauryan material culture were absorbed. The well being of the people was the prime importance to the kings and people were treated as their own children by the kings. The Satavahanas were Brahmins and ardent followers of Hinduism and their community was given an exalted status in the society. But the kings showed remarkable tolerance towards other religions like Buddhism. Endowments were made to Buddhist vihars and many Buddhist caves, chaityas and stupas were constructed. The Buddhist monks and the Brahmins were well respected and highly honoured and they also followed high moral conduct in their lives, true to the preaching of their respective religions. The Satavahana kings administered in accordance with principles of Dharma sastras and ancient divine traditions and did not consider themselves as divine and infallible. According to the economic activity and status, the society was divided into four classes. The family was the smallest unit of a society, as in ancient Hindu tradition and the eldest male member was the head of the family who was revered

---

6   Ajay Mitra Shastri, *The Satavahanas and the Western Kshatrapas: A historical framework* 197 (Dattsons, Pune, 1998).

and obeyed by the rest of the members. Elders were well taken care of. Women were respected. Mothers were placed on a high pedestal and occupied the altar of the society. It is s common for the kings to add the names of their mothers to their own name, like Gautamiputra, Vashishthiputra, Pulumavi and Kaushakiputra. It can be inferred that parents were shown their due deference and honour by the society during this period and the kings stood as testimony of this. Mothers took the guardianship of their minor sons and administered as their regents. Nashik cave inscription speaks of unchecked obedience of Gautamiputra Satakarni to his mother Gautami Balashri[7].

3.1.3. Gupta Dynasty

It is widely accepted that Sri Gupta was the first ruler of Gupta dynasty and succeeded by his son Maharaja Ghatotkacha. Some historians are of the opinion that Chandragupta I, who climbed the royal seat in 320 AD was the founder of Gupta imperial dynasty and he was followed by Samudragupta, an exceptional warrior and a ruler blessed with a keen political acumen. His kingdom extended throughout north India, from Himalayas to the Narmada River in South, from Punjab in the west and present Assam in the east. It is said that he travelled beyond present Chennai in the south, defeating kings en route and made them as fiduciaries of his vast kingdom that was the largest since Emperor Asoka's. The golden age of India, which has influenced and galvanized the later generations of Indians began during his period which reached its zenith during his successor Vikramaditya, Chandragupta II, who was a valorous son of a valiant father, a noble statesman,

---

7   C. K. Gairola, *A Cultural History of the Satavahana Dynasty* 271 (University of London, 1949).

able administrator and a patron of classical arts. He was followed by his son Kumaragupta who ruled for forty long years and maintained the prosperity and extent of the kingdom. After him, the empire started to weaken for numerous and diverse reasons and disintegrated into smaller kingdoms of various kings of Gupta lineage till eight century AD.

Resurrection of Hinduism took place during the Gupta period. Aswamedha yaga, an ancient custom of Hindu kings, was performed by many Gupta kings. It is said that the present and full forms of the two great epics, Ramayana and Mahabharata, have taken place during this period. Even the last phase of Smiriti was said to have been written during this dynasty. Vayu Purana, one of the eighteen puranas, was said to have taken its current shape during this period[8]. It was further said that orthodox rites and traditions were added to various sections of many puranas. Smiritis of Katayana, Devala and Vyasa were shown to belong to Gupta period and bhasya, the commentaries, to the various smiritis were also written. Even some historiographers place the Manu smiriti to this period. However it is also said smiriti laws were followed generally but not rigidly. The Hindu Brahmanical rites were encouraged in the form of endowments. Buddhism was the other dharmic religion that tried to regain its preponderance. The Gupta kings were staunch Hindus, but showed remarkable tolerance towards other religions. Samudragupta, Vikramaditya and other kings donated to construct Buddha vihars. They even had ministers and army commanders who were ardent followers of Buddhism. The Buddhist inscriptions reveal that these kings possessed catholicity in their religious notions.

---

8   R. D. Banerji, *The Age of the Imperial Guptas* 115 (Life Span Publishers & Distributors (Rakesh Pruthi), 2011).

Samudragupta and Chnadragupta II carried wise heads on their strong shoulders which enabled them to win hundred battles and had tender hearts besides their lungs which led them to peaceful quests for classical arts and well being of the people. Samudragupta's and Vikramaditya's period were known for cultural renaissance, especially, of fine arts though there were all round developments in all sectors . After a long interval of five centuries during which India endured political disintegration and foreign invasions of Huns and Kushanas , the Gupta period is known for its cultural, temporal, cerebral, conscientious and spiritual progress. Impressive developments and outstanding intellectual activities in art, science, literature, medicine, astronomy and mathematics were the hall mark of this Periclean Age of Indian history. It is also compared with the Elizabethan period of English history. A stagnant civilization does not broaden its intellectual horizon and the new vistas in art and culture do not get opened up and the promethean urge wanes. Indian's vibrant culture during the Gupta period was a result of interaction and influence of various new distinct cultures, a beneficial result of foreign incursions and rule. These influences resulted in a culture of new shape, power and vitality that promoted intellectual activities in many fields. Life during this period was happier than ever before and an inspired and fertile culture was existing during this Golden Prime of Indian history. Law and humanity judiciously blended together, resulting in the wise administration of justice.

Women during this period were expected, by Vatsayana, to be of sufficiently educated to make family budget, manage domestic expenditures, exercise self-restraint and efficiently govern household management. Women were found to be attending to the comforts of the husband, observe religious rites along with him, taking care of elders at home and honouring their commands. A trait that is still followed in Hindu families. The king was regarded as associated with divinity, but not with infallibility. He was expected to obey the elders in the society and cultivate righteousness, revering age-old customs and soliciting the prosperity of his subjects. The earlier Gupta kings were known for their compassion towards poor. For example samudragupta was keen on the support to the poor, destitute and helpless neglected people and elders. He was often compared to Indra and Varuna, the celestial Hindu Gods. He was very loving towards his father and his people at large. Though the people generally followed Hinduism, they were influenced by Buddhism also. Choultries and charity homes for travellers and wandering destitute for food and shelter, along the road sides as well as along out of the way roads were constructed by the people. Food, shelter and clothing were provided to monks. The Chinese traveller Fa-hien had remarked that affluent sections of the society built free hospitals for indigent and neglected patients, orphans, widows and disabled. Food and medicines were provided with free of cost to them.

Thus it can be enunciated that Vedic tradition of showing deference to the elders and parents, taking care of the poor and sick were prevalent throughout the Gupta period – the fag end of ancient period.

3.2. Filial and Elderly Care in India during Medieval Period

It is both interesting and depressing to ponder over the question 'whether there exists an unwritten reciprocal agreement or obligation' between the parents and children. Naturally, a responsibility lies to take care of another in turn which is the very basic notion of the parent-child relationship[9]. Sometimes, the dissection of the underlying reasons and rational behind human love could be embarrassing. The question is whether the grievance of parents over the unfortunate death of a child is due to the loss of the child or over the loss of future ministrations which the child was supposed to provide. Whether the succour provided to the aged parents is a result of pure untarnished love or a social obligation or simply a pay back of the care received from the parents earlier? In human beings, it is said to be a combination of both natural love and a reciprocal of earlier services[10]. The necessity of converting the filial love as a legal obligation during the ancient period in Rome and Greece points to an unfortunate circumstances of the parents during their dotage in that part of the world. During the medieval ages, there was no any such laws in Europe though the duty to take care of the aged parents and elders have largely been neglected. The aged parents entered into retirement contracts and leased their land properties to the strangers. In return, they were to be provided with grains and other sundry items like clothes, shoes etc.[11]. Even

---

9   G. Lambert, R. Rhetoric Rampant, *The Family under siege in the early Western Tradition* 91 (Faculty of Education, University of Western Ontario, London, 1982).

10 Josephine M. Cummins, *Attitudes to old age and ageing in medieval society* (2000) (Unpublished PhD. Thesis, University of Glasgow).

11 David Herlihy, "Age, Property, and Career in Medieval Society", in Michael M. Sheehan (eds.), *Aging and the Aged in Medieval Europe* 143 – 158 (Toronto: Pontifical Institute of Mediaeval Studies, 1990).

churches were involved in such types of contracts with aged land owners, providing care to them in return. It must be said that the western culture is not an ideal one. It promotes baser instincts in men in the name of individual freedom. This individuality and individual freedom are simply euphemisms for the self-serving nature of their culture, the pivot of which lies in their materialistic concepts. Fortunately, the eastern part of the world is an embodiment of virtuous cultural values where human feelings and co-existence were given a pedestal seat. The elders were treated with respect in medieval period in this part of the world, including India. At least there exists nothing in contrary to this belief.

The word medieval derives its origin from Latin and it means middle age. The Indian history which falls between 6th and 16th centuries is called medieval period of India. This period in turn is divided in to the early medieval period (AD 700 – AD 1200) and the late medieval period (AD 1200 – AD 1700). Thus this period lies as a bridge between ancient and modern periods. It starts from the end of Gupta dynasty and ends with the start of the decline of Mughal period. This period is characterised by the tumultuous times that India underwent. The country repeatedly experienced painful incursions and invasions by kings, despots, tyrants and nomad tribes from various parts of the world especially from central Asia and west Asia and Mongols in the north across Himalayas. Thus Turks, Afghans, Uzbeks, Turkmen, Mangolians and Persians ravaged the country and it continued ad infinitum. It must be said that Southern part of India did not suffer much from these and remained largely insulated, due to the Satpura, Maikal and Vindya ranges that divided the country, from these vicious upheavals and chaos.

During the early medieval period of Harsha and Hun dynasties and later medieval i.e. Maratha and Mughal period, the relationship within the societies remained the same without much change. The emotional bonding between all the members of the joint family was the grass root that held the system together. Though there have been constant turbulence and upheavals, they were of mostly political in nature and religious to some extent. However, the social structure largely remained unperturbed. The family structure was intact. At least there is nothing in evidence to suggest otherwise. The long rule of the Mughals in the late medieval period stabilized the Indian society and helped in uniting the people from different regions of India. The potpourri of various cultures and traditions that India is made, as of today, is because of these subjugations that the country was subjected to. People of different cultures, language and religions have settled in this country and have been absorbed into the mainstream. And their alien cultures, traditions and customs permeated the existing Hindu culture and a medley of various religions, cultures and languages started to coexist in India.

As far as Hinduism is concerned, it underwent major revival with the birth of Adi Sankaracharya during the early medieval period and Ramanuja, three centuries later. Bhakthi movement during the period under discussion brought changes and much needed reforms in the religion. The movement was spear headed by many sages and saint – poets who preached different philosophies. Saints like Chaitanya, Nanak, Meera, Kabir, Ramdas, Tulsi, Madvacharya, Ramanujar, Annamayya, Ramadoss, 64 Nayanmars, 12 Alwars and Tukaram were instrumental in the propagation of bhakthi movement in Hinduism. Local languages gained prominence in venerating and adoring the God, breaking the monopoly of Sanskrit. Because of this local language factor, the messages of the saints reached the common man and influenced them to great extents. A great number of temples were built and this had profound and positive influence of economy of the villages. This had a salutary effect on the way of living and ethos of the masses. There are extensive details about the social structure during this period. However, there is hardly any mention about the status of elders.

Whatever little materials that are available inform that the elders were treated with great care and respect. It has been stated that children showed respect and reverence to the parents and elders. Satananda, the well known astronomer of medieval Orissa, has said that the speck of dust from the feet of his father which he applied on his forehead has triggered the brilliance of his knowledge. Though it is a metaphor, it indicates how the parents were respected during the medieval period. Similarly, loyalty to husband, respect to aged, geniality to guests, devotion to gods, empathy and sympathy towards destitute and indigents were considered the hall marks of a good woman[12]. Since religion was the back bone of social behaviours, it is inferred that people took care of their parents as per the dictums in their religious scripts and Holy books. On the other hand, it is found that the filial piety of various kings of various dynasties is mentioned in the history annals.

3.2.1. Vardhana Dynasty

There are no solid details available regarding the exact year of establishment of Vardhana (Pushyabhuti) dynasty (Early Medieval Period). Harsha Vardhana (606-647 AD) was the most famous emperor of Vardhana dynasty. His empire covered most parts of

---

12 Mallick, Pravat Kumar, *Life in medieval Orissa* 1038 1568 A. D. (1989) (Unpublished Ph.D., Thesis, Sambalpur University).

northern India and spread up to river Narmada in the south. He ruled his kingdom from his capital Kanyakubja (present Kanauji in Uttar Pradesh).

Non-violence in the form of ban on the slaughter of animals was followed during Harsha regime. The poor and destitute were taken care by the kingdom. They were fed and their health requirements were attended to. Harsha Vardhana used to arrange massive religious assemblies at Prayag during the every fifth year of his rule and had attended six religious gatherings during his lifetime as a king. The custom he followed during each assembly was donating liberally all the wealth and savings of his kingdom. He did not spare even his personal belongings. He was very generous by giving away money, articles and ornaments and even his clothes to the poor, as per Hindu custom, during those assemblies. And he will cover his body from the cloth from his sister, after donating everything. All Indian dharmic faiths speak highly of charity. In India, charity and religion are inseparable. And usually the elders are the leading members of the society in helping the destitute. Hiuen Tsang, the Chinese traveller, has noted that the king Harsha constructed choultries (Punvashalas) along the highways of his empire. Food and stay were provided free of cost for travellers. Free medical care was provided to the poor and needy. Banabhatta, the famous author of his time, also lauded the welfare works of Harsha. It was said India was the most educated country during that time. All the three major religions viz. Hinduism, Buddhism and Jainism continued their sway over the people during the dynasty. All the three religions coexisted and religious tolerance was adhered to. Hinduism was the followed by majority of the people. There had not been any noteworthy changes in the culture and way of living of the people. The traditions, customs and values that were in existence during Gupta's dynasty were continued to be pursued during Vardhana dynasty also. Culture continuity was a notable feature of this dynasty[13]. From the welfare works of the emperor and culture followed by people, as evidenced by the above suggests that elders should have been well taken care by the children.

3.2.2. Chola Dynasty

After the disintegration of Harsha's empire, the country was ruled by many dynasties, but none of them could bring the entire Ganges valley under their rule. There were kalabhras empire in the south, Pala empire in the east, Pratihara empire in the west, Rastrakuta empire which dominated the Deccan as well as central India , Cholas in the south at various times before the country was invaded from the west Asia.

Cholas dynasty can be divided into two phases. Earlier Cholas dynasty was during Sangam period (600 BCE – 300 CE). Karikala cholan was the most prominent of them. The empire was known for prosperity and social justice. Also during the period of the king Kochenkannan, many beautiful temples, known for their grandeur, were built along the banks of the river Cauvery. He was one of the 63 Nayanmars who spread Shaivism. The society was steeped in respect for tradition, piety and social values and even the cruellest king would not have dared to harm the people. And as the popular saying goes, "yadha rajah, thadha praja, the elders would have been treated with respect and taken care of by their children following the footsteps of the kings.

---

13 Devika Rangachari, *Harsha Vardhana (Classics)* 48 (BSCHO Publications, Mumbai, 2009).

The later Cholas ruled over major part of south India starting from the year 848 A.D. for the next five hundred years. The kingdom was very prosperous. The kings initiated many social innovations and developments for the economic progress of poor and empowerment of women. Women also shared administrative responsibilities. The medieval period, particularly Cholas dynasty was known for building temples. These temples served not only religious purposes but also they were the community feeding centres for the destitute and children. The kingdom itself apportioned, along with the children, the obligation of maintenance of elders and the deprived segment of the society. The queens also took part not only in the construction of temples, but also in the welfare of the people. Sembian Maadevi was a queen who showed keen interest in the renewal of old and dilapidated temples. And the royal family established many hospitals. Princess Kundhavi, sister of Rajaraja Chola was instrumental in establishment of many hospitals for the elderly and the needy. Thus, the royal family stood at the forefront for taking care of ageing people. Also, education was given prime importance. Two colleges at Rajaraja Chadurvedi Mangalam and Thirubhuvam were functioning during the period of Rajendra Chola I. The Thiruvaaduthurai Mutt was running a school for medicine. The Thirumukkoodal temple, near Kanchi functioned as a temple, fully equipped hospital and a medical college.[14] Mutts and religious monasteries with the liberal support of kings developed into centres of learning and education. As a part of vocation training, the fathers passed on the mastery of their skills to their children.

---

14 Raghavan Srinivasan, *Rajaraja Chola: Interplay Between an Imperial Regime and Productive Forces of Society* 103 (One Point Six Technologies Pvt. Ltd. 1st edn., 2021).

This period was known for rapid development of classical art and civilisation. It was a period of prosperity, cultural growth and political prowess. Not to be left behind, bhakthi movement was at its peak during the Chola period. Bhakthi movement had far reaching economic, social and even political implications. It definitely moulded the social behaviour of the people. Nayanmars and Alwars who were born in various communities spearheaded in spreading the movement and these people associated with the religion have exercised enormous power and influence. And they preached that the moral behaviour is a precondition to attain salvation and also many of them stood examples of filial piety. The temples During Chola period functioned as centres for the development of arts and crafts. They functioned as learning centres for Holy Scriptures and Vedas. A salient feature of this period was the development of a temple oriented society. It was instrumental in the cultural, economic and cultural development of people[15]. It is not redundant to say that temples were associated with the progress of villages and towns in which they were situated, as today. It provided employment and accommodation to people in various strata of the society like sculptors, potters, blacksmiths, gardeners, washer men, idol makers, dancers, singers, weavers, doctors and Vedic Brahmins. The kings donated vast tracts of land for the maintenance of temples. Also wealthy people donated liberally to these temples. The temples functioned as economic centres. Since they were flush in funds, they lent money for traders. Thus, religion played a very great part in the lives of people in those periods.

The medieval Cholas period is known for deep religious fervour. The Cholas kings were passionate Shivaities and most of the temples

---

15 K. A. Nilakanta Sastri, *A History Of South India (Oip): From Prehistoric Times To the Fall of Vijayanagar* 91 (Oxford University Press, 1st edn., 1997).

belonged to this sect of Hinduism. Shaivism was the most followed sect during those periods in Cholas Kingdom. In Shavism, Lord Shiva and His consort are called 'Ammaiyappar'. It means that they shower love on the devotees as a mother and father would on their child. It shows how the parents are offered a very high pedestal in those days. They are equated with the God. Similarly, Lord Shiva is also known as 'Thayumanavar'. It means that He is both a father and a mother. It further explains the fact that parents are seated at the highest altar. A reasonable doubt may arise that whether a religion can lead the lives of people. It has been proven many times that religion is an inseparable part of the people in those days. Why, even today, it is for a majority of the people. Hinduism, particularly, shaped the life of the people in this country and is intertwined with the thought process of the people and gives a meaning to their lives. It shaped up the destiny of the nation as a whole. The religious preaching have profound effect on the way the people think and behave. It has a dominant influence on the way of living of the people. Hence, combined with the historical evidences, it can be inferred that elders, parents and necessitous people were taken care during Cholas regime.

The later part of medieval period in India is said to be a period of Turkish and Mogul rule over the country. However, history of this great country is not just rise and fall of various dynasties without any economical and cultural growth. Emergence of great dynasties, establishment of a vast empire and their final disintegration leading to the rise of a new dynasty was a cyclical process. In spite of these political upheavals, the country continued to be progress economically and culturally.

3.2.3. Maratha Dynasty

The great filial love, in a royal family, showed by Shivaji Maharaj towards his mother Jijabhai is unparalleled in the history of India. She was instrumental for the rise of the Maratha dynasty and the revival of the hope among Hindus who were reeling under the tyranny of Mogul kings. Due to unfortunate chain of circumstances, the father was separated from his wife and son. It was the mother who single handedly brought up her son, warped him into a great warrior and made him to envision an independent Hindu swarajya free from the fetters of Mogul dynasty. However, much is not much written in the history books about the child-parent love between Maharaj Shivaji and his father Shahaji who was working in the council of Bijapur sultan, the archenemy of Shivaji. The author narrates in great detail the reunion of father and son after many years.[16] The love and respect shown by Shivaji was emblematic of the typical Indian, steeped in its traditions and culture.

The father was received by Shivaji along with his the cavalry, elephants and foot soldiers amid much fanfare, jubilation and music. The son prostrated, as in the truly Hindu tradition, before his father who in turn raised him up and embraced, joyful tears drenching the cheeks. The son walked bare-footed holding the footwear of his father in his hand while the father was raiding in a palanquin. Upon the arrival to his place, the son stood obediently before the seated father, still holding the slippers in hand. With great reverence, the son explained and prayed for his understanding of the circumstances under which he was forced to wage war with Bijapur. The son also prayed for forgiveness from the father for having put his life in danger and was ready to undergo any punishment, if any, if the

---

16 N. S. Takakhav, *The life of Shivaji Maharaj* 73 (Manoranjan press, Mumbai, 3rd edn., 2008).

father deems fit. The father was so overwhelmed and felt proud over the valour and the achievements of his son. The son felt happy at these encouraging words, bowed down at the feet of his father and said that he was just instrumental and the all the glory belonged to the father. Such was the, humility, devotion and reverence of Shivaji Maharaj towards his father though he alone, save for his mother's encouragement, was the sole reason for the establishment of the Maratha kingdom.

The son, as a mark of the joyful event, gave donations to the poor. During his stay at Shivaji's place, the father and his entourage were treated with utmost respect and hospitality and Shivaji personally made sure of the comforts of his father. During the stay of the father, all state affairs were conducted with his permission, as a mark of respect and honour. Shivaji, in spite of being the architect of a Hindu nation, was such a humble son who showed enormous devotion and deference to his father. The delighted father presented his own sword to his son as a show of affection and Shivaji received it with great revere and respect and kept this sword by the side of his own sword 'Bhavani'. He worshipped both of them during ordinary times. The son diligently took care of his step-mother also during her stay. The advice of the experienced father in the strengthening of Maratha army, forts and on the war equipments was sought by the son. On the father's departure to Bijapur, Shivaji was very emotional and asked, but in vain, the father to stay at his place during his old age in the tranquil calm of his own place rather than spending at Bijapur. The son requested the servants, of his father to take care of him properly because of his dotage, assuring them of rewards. It is said that the father extracted an agreement from the son not to further attack Bijapur, as long as he was alive. Shivaji relented from his principle for his father and did not attack Bijapur till his father's demise as per wishes. Shivaji was devastated on the death of his beloved father and grieved that he lost his protector. He lamented that his father's tacit support, approval, appreciation and pride on his exploits were the driving forces behind his conquests over the Muslim dynasties. The much distressed Jijabhai decided to perform sati and the crestfallen Shivaji begged her to refrain from doing so. Only the realization that Shivaji would not outlive her death and the Hindu rajya which was built up painstakingly for many years would collapse desisted her from the earlier decision and she remained a grieving widow. Shivaji Maharaj spent enormously for the final funeral rites of his father. Such was Shivaji's love for his father in spite of the fact the father had abandoned the parental duty of bringing up the son. He built a monument in honour of his deceased father and donated villages for its maintenance. There was an immense and stupendous difference in the characters of Shivaji and Aurangazeb, his peer. The latter had killed his own brothers and incarcerated his own biological ageing father till his death to usurp the throne. Shivaji also slained Ghorpade, a treachery figure and who was instrumental in the downfall of Shahaji and fulfilled another of his filial duties. Shivaji Maharaj's love towards his parents was an embodiment of Hindu culture and he performed his filial duties, even compromising and sacrificing his political goals.

3.2.4. Mogul Dynasty

Though there are scant materials available on the status of elders of the common class in the medieval India, there are many stories and anecdotes available about the filial piety and poignant parent-child relationships in the royal families of Mogul dynasty. During those times, it was presumed that an illness could be transferred, by means of strong prayers and donations, from one person to another. The Mogul prince Humayun was on his death bed with an inexplicable illness. When his health deteriorated in spite of the best efforts of the court physicians, Babur, his father and the king, resorted to prayers and appealed to the Almighty to intervene and transfer the illness to him. It was believed that due to this selfless prayers combined with the extraordinary love towards his son, Humayun's health improved and simultaneously Babur's health weakened leading to this death. It was stated in Humayun –Nama that Babur has prayed, "if a life can be exchanged for a life, I who am Babur give my own life and being in exchange for my son". This heart-rending story is a weighty and a strong proof of a parent's love towards his son.[17]

During later years, the king Akbar built a beautiful and exquisite tomb in remembrance of his deceased father Humayun in Delhi in the 1560s. The garden-tomb was first of its kind in mogul dynasty built in Persian style. The garden setting was an inspiration from the description of heaven in the Islamic Holy book Quran. The grandeur and magnificence of this tomb was a precursor to the construction of Taj Mahal which was built 80 years later. This mausoleum is later called as the necropolis of the dynasty where more than 150 members of the royal families were buried. The tomb stands as a testament to Akbar's filial piety. In Ain-i-Akbari, its famous author Abu'l Fazl has stated that Akbar has lamented over the early demise of his father Humayun because of which Akbar was robbed of the opportunity to show reverence to his father.[18]

---

17 Ram Sharma, "The Story of Babar's Death", *The Journal of the Royal Asiatic Society of Great Britain and Ireland* 295-298 (1926).

18 Glenn D. Lowry, IV *Humayun's Tomb: Form, Function, and Meaning in Early Mughal Architecture* 133-148 (Brill Open Soc. Sci., 1987).

Another indubitable structure of filial love, in the Mogul dynasty, is the It-ma-ud-Daula that exists in the city of Agra, which competes with Taj Mahal for its elegance and grandeur. It was built by the Mogul Empress, Nur Jahan, wife of Jahangir, for her demised father, Mirza Ghias. Such was her unparalleled love towards her father that, initially, she thought of constructing this monument in pure silver and was dissuaded by her brother to use white marble on the fear of plunder. This magnificent edifice stands, constructed in 1631, as a corroboration of her love towards her father. After becoming the empress of the dynasty, she had seen to that both her father and brother occupied high offices in the court of Jahangir. Also she has strengthened the relationship of her brother by marrying of his daughter to the heir apparent, Khurram – later known as Shah Jahan. This monument, a tribute to a father, stands on the bank of river Jamuna and is a resplendent example of ornamentation that was used in the construction.[19]

Not be left behind and matching to the filial love of his wife, the emperor Jahangir showered great admiration and veneration towards his biological as well as foster mother. It is stated that he used to wait upon his mother after coming out of his Lahore fort.[20] His passionate and warm meeting with his foster mother, after crossing the river in a boat, near Lahore has been explained in his memoirs, "Tuzuk–i–Jahangir (vol 1, p 76). Jahangir narrates how he paid his reverence to her and prostrated before her. He became distressed on her death. He placed the feet of the deceased foster

---

19 K. R. N. Swamy, "A mughal empress' tribute to her father", *The Sunday Tribune*, Dec. 02, 2001, *available at* <https://www.tribuneindia.com/2001/20011202/spectrum/main3.htm> (last accessed on May 07, 2025).

20 Sehar Khwaja, Fosterage and Motherhood in the Mughal Harem: Intimate Relations and the Political System in Eighteenth-Century India, 46 *Journal of Social Scientist* 39-60 (2018).

mother on his shoulders and carried the corpse. He was so dejected that he refused his food and did not change his clothes.[21] Another extraordinary filial love shown in the same dynasty belongs to the admirable and docile Princess Jahanara, daughter of Shah Jahan, towards her father. After the demise of his wife Mumtaj, the emperor was so distressed and grief stricken that he gradually lost his will in the administration of kingdom. His daughter had taken over the administration of royal zenna at an early age of 17 and devoted her life to serve and take care of her distressed father. She renounced her love life, against wishes of her family members, so as to discharge her responsibility towards him. Also her efforts to unite the warring family members did go in vain.[22]

Aurangazeb is all along known for his cruelty, religious prejudice, fratricidal behaviours and patricidal tendencies. However, there is a valiant attempt to justify his actions and calling him a very devoted son. The authors have mentioned that he was a faithful and loyal son, in spite of the great iniquities meted out to him by his father Shah Jahan. He informed in one of his many such letters to his sister Jahanara that he was ready to die if their father wishes so and was ready to lead to life of humility if he was ordered so by their father. Even when the elderly father was put under guard, the authors stated that he was treated well with sympathy and respect. The dutiful son used to meet him often and present gifts, the authors said. The authors went on to add that even Shah

---

21 Henry Beveridge, I *The Tuzuk-i-Jahangiri or Memoirs of Jahangir: From the First to the Twelfth Year of His Reign* 84 – 85 (Manohar Publishers & Distributors, 2015).

22 Indu Sundaresan, "A whip of the glorious past", *The New Indian Express*, Nov 22, 2010, *available at* <https://www.newindianexpress.com/education/edex/2010/nov/22/a-whiff-of-the-glorious-past-204961.html> (last accessed on May 07, 2025).

Jahan was satisfied with the treatment. Since Aurangazeb was very religious and a pious man, it was argued that he would not have done any harm nor showed disrespect towards his father against the edicts mentioned in Quran or Hadith. He followed the filial duty mentioned in the Holy book by obeying Shah Jahan's flawed orders, even if they were harmful to him. He was a true Muslim for he was not resentful towards his father though he was subjected to many injustices by Shah Jahan.[23]

---

23 Quazi Nurul Hamim & Sk Mohammad Hasan, "Aurangazeb's veneration for father – Distorted or reality" 1 *Universe International Journal of Interdisciplinary Research* 29 (2021).

3.3. Filial and Elderly Care in India during Modern Period

The later or modern generations have the advantage of viewing the world by being perched on the shoulders of the ancestors and gain a greater field of vision than the elders and become more knowledgeable. That does not mean that the former are more intelligent than the latter. It is because of the wisdom the children gained from the experiences of the ancestors. By the use of the term 'modern', it has become possible to compare the new concepts with the older ones. It enables the new generation to self analyse how far it is able to visualise beyond what already existed. This is a continuous process and as the culture keeps progressing, newer concepts keep evolving due to this exercise. This helps to understand and differentiate between traditional and modern views. It enables to analyse how the system and culture have progressed through temporal changes. These changes can be conveniently studied as pertaining to ancient, medieval and modern periods.

3.3.1. During British Regime

India is a country of collection of amazing numbers and varieties of traditions and cultures. It is a collage of various ethnic, linguistic, religious, caste and community diversities which are so different in most aspects of life. These diversities crisscross the Indian society with an astonishing level of mutual tolerance and co-existence. The single nation-state society is so multifaceted that it is equivalent to that of the entire European continent. In spite of so many sub-cultures, the common basic themes that are running undercurrent in all of them are the reasons for the social harmony that is not witnessed anywhere in the world. Whatever be the cultural virtues of India, the onset of colonialism destroyed many ethos of the country that it carried for centuries. The most important of them was the care and respect to the parents and elders.

An inherent characteristic of Hindu family is the utmost care taken by the parents and elders on the children and vice versa. It was made possible because of the nature of the family set up as spelt out in Hinduism. It will be pertinent to highlight the joint family system which remains an essential part of a Hindu family which was the first casualty with the beginning of British dominance in the 18th century. It has been stated that the colonial laws did not try to interfere with the social life, religious attitude and traditions of British India. It is a well known fact that a wilful cooperation of the common man is an imperative for the success of a social legislation. In this regard, the East India Company failed to educate properly on the viciousness of the some of the abhorrent customs that were prevailing during those days, before banning those practices. After the first independence war off 1857, which the British preferred to be called as sepoy mutiny, the government at London was of the opinion that the mutiny was a result of East India Company's interference in the traditions and customs of native Indians, especially, interference in child marriages and the banning of sati in 1829. When India came under the rule of British crown, it was assured that colonial authorities would refrain from meddling with the religious persuasions of Indians. It was thought that colonial government's views on the traditions of India stopped at the doorstep of Indian household. But in reality, the British attempted to influence the way of living of India, albeit furtively to avoid any religious backlashes.

The institution of family came under enormous pressure by the reforms of Macaulay in the education system. The church also aided in the spread of modern education. The children were slowly pulled away from their traditional systems and came into contact with western culture. It must be said that, initially, the number was small and hence the effect of westernisation was gradual.[24] There was a gradual incursion of the materialistic attitude of western civilisation and colonising culture. Modernisation caprices have led the men in a particular section of the society, who were working under the British government, to ape the western culture and a slow withering away of the joint family system started to take its roots. An alien licentious life style emerged and permeated through the Indian society among the educated class. A slow and gradual erosion of moral values that were the hall marks of Indian culture took place. Reverence to elders and the joint family system were some of the earliest victims of this degradation of the culture. The joint family system, which was the basic tenet of the Indian society slowly disintegrated and the concept of nuclear family entered to remain forever in India. The individual was more perturbed about himself and his immediate family. He became self-centred and his duty to the society was relegated to the back seat. And his obligation to the parents and elders who were in need of care and attention was given scant respect. His attitude towards them turned to apathy as if their lives were expendable and meeting their needs was of no importance and it did not find a place in his all important self progress. It was a regression towards the period of beginning of human race. The parents and elders were consigned to the margins and were left to subsist and survive on their own. What started as a trickle at the beginning soon morphed into tsunami and this negligent culture has spread its tentacles deep into and throughout the society, irrespective of faith and caste and community.

---

24 Antoinette Burton, *Dwelling in the Archive: Women Writing House, Home, and History in Late Colonial India* 114 (Oxford University Press, U.S.A. 2003).

3.3.2. After Independence

The world has witnessed massive changes and advances in technology and science during the last two centuries, as a result of which there had been a great social metamorphosis. This change in the social character had its genesis in Western Europe and North America, since much of the technological advancements and industrialisation originated in that part of the world. At the same time, there was a gradual increase in the percentage of elderly people due to advancements in medical field which resulted in the increase in the longevity of human life. The modernisation led to creation of new roles for the common man and there began a considerable change in the status of the older people. The western world switched its structure from an agrarian and bucolic nation into industrialized countries and there was a complete transfiguration of the society accordingly. As the nation and the society became more prosperous, the social displacement caused by the migration of the people altered the social structure.

After the Second World War, the non – industrialised countries were also encouraged to convert from being agriculture based to industrialised by following the footsteps of western nations. Modernisation of these traditionally conservative countries replaced their traditional institutions, which were considered roadblocks to developments. The societies were gently and indirectly goaded to discord their culture and customs which were regarded as anti modern and illiberal. The term modernisation originated in the western world and gathered prominence after the Great War in 1940s. It alludes to a set of events and changes in the society during the process of industrialization in that part of the world. It can be seen that the modernisation had profound effect on the lives of senior citizens throughout the world. The position of the elders were influenced by tremendous progress in health sector, changes in the economic status as a result of modernisation, migration to urban areas in search of livelihood as a result of industrialisation and rapid advancements in the field of education. As said earlier, the advancements in the medical field has improved the health of the population and increased the life span. However, due to this increase in the longevity, the elder people lost preference in the labour market because of more competition. With the rapid industrialization, newer technologies were developed to augment production. The newer technologies mean newer and greater opportunities for the people who acquire the latest skills. The younger generation was at the forefront in mastering over the newer techniques and this vibrant younger generation, with the latest work skills became the preferred workforce, consigning the elders to jobs with lesser pay scale or into early retirement. In many instances they found themselves with the pink slips. This led to a loss of income and thereby loss of honour and respect resulting in the lowering of social status. Now, the elders became dependents and there was a reversal of roles unlike in a conventional society in which elders were the controlling authorities in the family. This eroded the status of the seniors in the family and in the society[25].

Thus, the British rule and modernisation has resulted in the disintegration of joint family system and paved the way for nuclear families which in turn resulted in decline of role of senior citizens in the family.

---

25 A. W. Achenbaum, *Old Age in the New Land* 52 – 65 (Johns Hopkins University Press, 1978).

Part – C

Legal Perspective

CHAPTER – 4

Filial and Elderly Care – Legal Perspective

Introduction

In India, several measures were taken to provide basic necessities for senior citizens. Adarkar commission in 1944 even before independence has submitted a report on elderly problem. Providence compelled our constitution framers to include provisions to make elderly population to breathe easier. In order to promote well-being, to take care of the basic necessities and keeping up with the assurances to elderly population, the well-being of senior citizens is mandated in the Constitution of India under Article 41[1]. The said provision falls under Part IV of the constitution, i.e. Directive Principles. Thus, the Constitutional makers have felt the necessity of protecting the interests and well – being of the elderly and incorporated a provision for them under the Constitution of India.

After independence, the law makers have enacted the Hindu Adoption and Maintenance Act (HAMA) in the year 1956 under which a provision was incorporated for providing maintenance to

---

1   Article **41. Right to work, to education and to public assistance in certain cases:** The State shall, within the limits of its economic capacity and development, make effective provision for securing the right to work, to education and to public assistance in cases of unemployment, old age, sickness and disablement, and in other cases of undeserved want.

parents. This legislation is applicable only to Hindus and people belonging to other faith have their separate personal laws and hence HAMA has not brought much effect in the Indian society. In order to overcome this, provision for maintenance has been incorporated under Section 125 of the Criminal Procedure Code in the year 1973 which is applicable to all persons irrespective of their personal laws. Though the concept of 'Maintenance' is a civil remedy, the law makers have incorporated the same into criminal law in order to give remedy to the maintenance seekers.

In spite of the existence of these filial support laws which cast a legal obligation to support the parents and other dependants since late fifties of last century, the abuses on parent's rights continued unabated. Hopes were belied since these Acts have failed to address the concerns of the elderly in a satisfactory manner and this resulted in the enactment of Maintenance and Welfare of Parents and Senior Citizens Act in the year 2007 exclusively for parents and senior citizens. The legislative measures taken to protect the rights of senior citizens in India after independence are discussed in this part briefly.

4.1. Personal Laws

Since the society has become a more unethical, discriminative and immoral cesspool as far the care to the elderly is concerned, the government has assumed the role of a wingman and came to the rescue of the elders by various legal provisions it has enacted. Various statutory provisions, under personal laws as well as under criminal code, were enacted culminating in legal responsibility on the children to take care of their parents and elders.

The tradition and culture of all communities impose a moral duty on the children to take care of their parents and elders. However, as per the laws, the extent of that commitment varies and dependant on the personal laws of the individual community.

4.1.1. Hindu Laws

The obligation on the sons to look after the welfare of their parents and elders have been emphasised even from Vedic days and the scriptures have repeatedly reiterated the said duty. In the year 1941, The Indian Government appointed a Hindu Law committee to look into the Women's Right to Property Act, 1937 to make amendments, under the chairmanship of B.N. Rao. The committee made suggestions for the reforms in Hindu Law also. As a result, many personal laws were enacted after independence to introduce reforms as well as make it uniform throughout the country. The Hindu Adoption and Maintenance Act (HAMA) in the year 1956 was one among them. HAMA was made applicable to anyone who

1. Is a Hindu by religion in any of its forms or development
2. Practices Jainism, Sikhism and Buddhism
3. Is a legitimate or illegitimate child of born to parent(s) of either of the above-mentioned religions or so brought up

4. Is a legitimate or illegitimate or abandoned or child of unknown parentage brought up as a Hindu or Jain or Sikh or Buddhist.

5. Is a child converted into either of these religions.

However, the Act does not apply to a Muslim or Christian or Parsi or Jew and those persons are governed by their individual religious personal laws. Provisions of this law are not available to a non-Hindu. The expression 'Maintenance' under the HAMA denotes provision for food, shelter, clothing, education and healthcare. The last word includes medical treatment as well as medical attendance. Section 20[2] of the HAMA states that a Hindu person has a duty to maintain his legitimate or illegitimate children and his aged or infirm parents, during his life time. This law is applicable to and so casts a duty on both men and women. The word 'parent' includes a childless step-mother also. However, it is unambiguously stated that this duty exists only when the aged or infirm parent is unable to maintain themselves out of their own earnings or property. Section 23[3] empowers the Court to decide whether any maintenance should be awarded to the claimant. Also, it is left

---

2   **S. 20. Maintenance of children and aged parents:** (1) Subject to the provisions of this section a Hindu is bound, during his or her lifetime, to maintain his or her legitimate or illegitimate children and his or her aged or infirm parents.

(2) A legitimate or illegitimate child may claim maintenance from his or her father or mother so long as the child is a minor.

(3) The obligation of a person to maintain his or her aged or infirm parent or a daughter who is unmarried extends in so far as the parent or the unmarried daughter, as the case may be, is unable to maintain himself or herself out of his or her own earnings or other property.

Explanation — In this section "parent" includes a childless step-mother.

3   **S. 23. Amount of Maintenance:** (1) It shall be in the discretion of the Court to determine whether any, and if so what, maintenance shall be awarded under the provisions of this Act, and in doing so, the Court shall have due

to the discernment and discretion of the Court to decide on the quantum of maintenance, if there is any. A word of caution is that this judgment of the Court should be based on sound principles of law. It should not be whimsical or impulsive. The decision should be in tune with the objectives of Act and is bound by the provisions of various sections in the enactment. During the course of deciding on the maintenance amount to the wife, children and aged and infirm parents, the Court should follow considerations like status and position of the claimants, the reasonable wants, whether the claimant is justified to claim maintenance, if he or she is residing alone from the respondent, the claimant's own earning, his other

---

regard to the considerations set out in sub-section (2), or sub-section (3), as the case may be, so far as they are applicable.

(2) In determining the amount of maintenance, if any, to be awarded to a wife, children or aged or infirm parents under this Act, regard shall be had to—
   (a) the position and status of the parties;
   (b) the reasonable wants of the claimant;
   (c) if the claimant is living separately, whether the claimant is justified in doing so;
   (d) the value of the claimant's property and any income derived from such property, or from the claimant's own earnings or from any other source;
   (e) the number of persons entitled to maintenance under this Act.

(3) In determining the amount of maintenance, if any, to be awarded to a dependant under this Act, regard shall be had to—
   a. the net value of the estate of the deceased after providing for the payment of his debts;
   b. the provision, if any, made under a will of the deceased in respect of the dependant;
   c. the degree of relationship between the two;
   d. the reasonable wants of the dependant;
   e. the past relations between the dependant and the deceased;
   f. the value of the property of the dependant and any income derived from such property, or from his or her earnings or from any other source;
   g. the number of dependants entitled to maintenance under this Act.

sources of income and total value of his properties, the number of claimants who are eligible to be awarded with maintenance, as per the Act etc. Section 24[4] bars anyone who is not a Hindu or ceased to be Hindu by his conversion to a different faith to claim maintenance under this Act. As a corollary to the Section 2 of the Act, the Section 24 reiterates that a person cannot demand any maintenance under this Act if he has ceased to be a Hindu by his conversion to a different religion. Section 25[5] deals with the alterations in maintenance amount under changed conditions. Alteration in the maintenance amount is permissible if materially changed circumstances justify a change in the maintenance amount which was fixed earlier either by Court or agreement between the parties.

Thus, the modern personal Hindu law to take care of the parents, The Hindu Adoption and Maintenance Act 1956, the first personal law in India in this regard, converted the earlier moral duty into a statutory obligation that can be enforced by the State. This duty is not dependant on possession of any family property. The said provision which casts a duty on the children to maintain their parents is placed in the Section 20 of the Act along with maintenance to children. It is to be noted that both the sons and daughters have equal duty to maintain their parents. The salient point of the Act is that only those parents who are financially incompetent to look after themselves, from any known sources of income, are eligible to plead for assistance from their children.

---

4   **S. 24. Claimant to maintenance should be a Hindu:** No person shall be entitled to claim maintenance under this Chapter if he or she has ceased to be a Hindu by conversion to another religion.

5   **S. 25. Amount of maintenance may be altered on change of circumstances:** The amount of maintenance, whether fixed by a decree of court or by agreement, either before or after the commencement of this Act, may be altered subsequently if there is a material change in the circumstances justifying such alteration.

4.1.2. Muslim Laws

The personal Muslim Law also casts a duty on the children to maintain their parents. As per the Law, even if the parents are able to earn by themselves, their children in easy circumstances are bound to take care of them. If the mother is poor, even if she is not infirm, the law places an obligation on the son, who may be in strained circumstances also, to maintain her. An earning son, whether he is poor or not, has to maintain his unearning father. According Hanafi Law, the children and grandchildren are obligated to maintain their indigent parents and grandparents. Both sons and daughters have this duty cast on them. However, this responsibility is dependent on their ability and means to do so.

4.1.3. Christian and Parsi Laws

The people following these faiths do not have personal laws that commit children to maintain their parents and the elders. The way out for the maintenance aspiring parents of the said faiths is to apply under the provisions of Criminal law, i.e., Section 144 of Bharatiya Nagarik Suraksha Sanhita, 2023 (Section 125 of CrPC, 1973).

4.2. Criminal Law

Initially there was no provision under CrPC to claim maintenance for parents. The Law Commission, initially, was not inclined to this proposal. It argued that the summary proceeding of this nature will make it difficult for the Court to apportion the maintenance amount among the children. It advised the policy makers to leave the job of adjudication to the civil Courts. Section 125 which was later introduced into the Code enabled the parents, who are not able to maintain themselves, to claim maintenance from their sons and daughters. The provision has laid the onus on the parents to show that the children have sufficient means to provide them succour. Even married daughters are liable to provide support to parents, under BNSS (Section 125 of CrPC).

Section 144(1)(d)[6] of the BNSS states that the person, who is having sufficient means, either neglects or refuses to maintain his

---

6   **S. 144. Order for maintenance of wives, children and parents:** (1) If any person having sufficient means neglects or refuses to maintain

    (d) his father or mother, unable to maintain himself or herself,

A Magistrate of the first class may, upon proof of such neglect or refusal, order such person to make a monthly allowance for the maintenance of his wife or such child, father or mother, at such monthly rate as such magistrate thinks fit, and to pay the same to such person as the Magistrate may from time to time direct:

Provided further that the Magistrate may, during the pendency of the proceeding regarding monthly allowance for the maintenance under this Sub-Section, order such person to make a monthly allowance for the interim maintenance of his wife or such child, father or mother, and the expenses of such proceeding which the Magistrate considers reasonable, and to pay the same to such person as the Magistrate may from time to time direct:

Provided also that an application for the monthly allowance for the interim maintenance and expenses of proceeding under the second proviso shall, as far as possible, be disposed of within sixty days from the date of the service of notice of the application to such person.

father and mother who are unable to maintain themselves, shall be directed by a first class magistrate, upon proof of such neglect or refusal, to provide a monthly allowance towards the maintenance of his father and mother. In the original CrPC 1973, the maximum monthly allowance was fixed at Rs 500 and this limitation was removed in the later amended version in the year 2001. The allowance amount, depending upon the facts and circumstances of the case, shall be fixed at the discretion of the magistrate and this allowance shall be paid to the father or mother from time to time as ordered by the magistrate. The word 'any person' in this section denotes only an individual but includes a person belonging to a joint undivided family. However, the proceedings shall be against the individual only and not against the joint undivided family. The joint family property may, however, be taken into consideration by the Magistrate to decide on the quantum of maintenance, if any granted. The section 144(1) (d) lays down some conditions for claiming maintenance by the parents. Either of parents should be unable to maintain by themselves. Also the person against whom the claim is made must have sufficient means or resources to support/maintain his parents and have chosen to neglect or refuse to maintain them. Neglect has the dictionary meaning of not to give enough care or attention to people or things that are one's responsibility. While neglect has a meaning of either an omission or a default when there is no demand, the word refusal comes into play when there is a failure or denial of a duty to maintain after such a demand[7]. Both neglect and refusal may be either express or implicit. And can be either by words or by conduct[8]. Both carry a connotation that they are more than simple failure or omission. The sweep and extent of refusal or neglect varies according to the dependent. If it is a wife,

---

7 *Narayan Sahu v. Sushama Sahu And Anr.,* 1992 Cri LJ 2912, Orissa HC.
8 *Bhikaiji Maneckji v. Maneckji Mancherji,* (1907) 9 Bom LR 359, Bombay HC.

neglect or refusal means something more than a failure or omission and the husband must clearly deny the maintenance to her to be called a refusal. If it is his child, a mere failure or omission can called be neglect or refusal. As per the old Section 488, the neglect or refusal must be in praesenti which means at the time of proceeding before the Magistrate[9].

Though the concept of maintenance of dependents falls under the category of civil remedy, the statute has been included in criminal law. The proceedings under the section 144 of the BNSS are not trail in nature and non-payment of maintenance is not considered as a criminal offence. It should not be construed that it is a punishment on the person against whom an order for maintenance is passed under this section for his past neglect or failure to maintain. The objective of its inclusion in the criminal law is to provide a simplified – devoid of all complex procedures involved in a similar civil right – speedy, but limited, relief to the claimants of maintenance and to make the procedure a summary in nature. The jurisdiction of the Criminal Court under this section is independent of and auxiliary to that of a Civil Court.

---

9   *Chand Begum* v. *Hyderabaig,* 1972 Cri LJ 1270, Andhra HC.

4.3. Maintenance and Welfare of Parents and Senior Citizens Act, 2007

From the beginning of this century, the Government of India is showing its concern for the benefit, maintenance, protection and welfare of senior citizens so that they can live a peaceful and harmonious life. It has formulated many policies, programmes and schemes for the welfare of older persons. Finally, the Government of India has enacted a welfare legislation in the year 2007 titled "Maintenance and Welfare of Parents and Senior Citizens (MWPSC) Act, 2007". For the protection and benefit of senior citizens this is the first direct legislation in Indian legal system.

The MWPSC Act defines a senior citizen as any person being a citizen of India, who has attained the age of sixty years or above[10]. The implementation of the Act comes under the domain of state governments and they are empowered under Section 32(1) to frame rules for the said purpose. They are authorised to appoint Maintenance Officers under Section 18(1) and to constitute Maintenance and Appellate Tribunals under Sections 7(1) and 15(1) respectively. The Act states that any person, under whose care is the senior citizen is, who intentionally abandons senior citizen is punishable with a maximum of three months of incarceration or with a maximum fine of five thousand rupees or both[11]. The state government shall give wide publicity through public media about the provisions of this Act[12]. The Act empowers the state governments put the District Magistrate in charge of duties and to ensure that the provisions of the Act are carried

---

10 S. 2(h) of Maintenance and Welfare of Parents and Senior Citizens (MWPSC) Act, 2007.
11 S. 24 of MWPSC Act, 2007.
12 S. 21 of MWPSC Act, 2007.

out, after endowing him with necessary powers[13]. The District Magistrate can, in turn, order a subordinate officer to excise these duties.

As per section 2(a) of the MWPSC Act, the term children include a son, daughter, grandson and grand – daughter. As per the Act, maintenance includes provision for food, clothing, residence and medical attendance and treatment[14]. While defining the term maintenance, the law makers have intentionally attached and placed broad connotation to prevent any narrow interpretation or construction[15]. Section 2(g)[16] of the Act define the term 'relative'. In the case of children, the obligation to maintain their parents is not conditional on being in possession of property of their parent or being a natural heir or upon a right of future inheritance. A childless senior citizen may avail the care from an institutionalised care centres such as old age homes. However, the warmth and love that one draws from near and dear may be missing in such institutions. Hence, the legislature has transferred the duty of their maintenance to a relative. The obligation to maintain a senior citizen rests on being a legal heir or in possession of property or would inherit the property of the senior citizen. If any of the above requirements are absent or if the senior citizen is indigent, the relative is not legally bound to maintain the senior citizen.

---

13 S. 22(1) of MWPSC Act, 2007.
14 S. 2(b) of MWPSC Act, 2007.
15 *Parmar Dahyabhai Hemabhai* v. *Parmar Prakashbhai,* Special Civil Application No. 4038 of 2011, decided on March 04, 2013, (Gujarat HC).
16 S. 2(g) "Relative" means any legal heir of the childless senior citizen who is not a minor and is in possession of or would inherit his property after his death.

4.3.1. Procedure and Jurisdiction for Claiming Maintenance

Any grandparent, parent including a senior citizen incapable of maintaining himself from his own earning or his property, can claim maintenance from one or more of his grandchildren or children as the case may be under this Act[17]. As per section 4(1), the claimant for maintenance needs to make an application under Section 5 to the tribunal. In the case of children, the maintenance obligation towards parents is not conditional on being in possession of the property of their parents or upon a right of possible future inheritance. The only condition is that the parent should be incapable of maintaining himself from his earning or any income from his property. In case of relative, the obligation to provide maintenance exists only if there is possibility of inheritance from the senior citizen.

The procedures for application for maintenance has been mentioned under Section 5. A parent or senior citizen may make an application for his maintenance by himself or by any other duly authorised person or organisation if he is incapable of doing that or the Tribunal itself may take cognizance sua motu[18]. Section 8 of the Act makes it tacitly clear that the procedure of enquiry to be held, as indicated in sub-section (3) of Section 5, shall be summary in nature. The maintenance plea is to be disposed from ninety days of the date of the application. Under exceptional circumstances, the tribunal is permitted to extend it by another thirty days. The legislation, to alleviate the sufferings of the elderly, has empowered the tribunal to order the respondents to pay a monthly interim allowance to the applicants while the application is in abeyance

---

17   S. 4(1)(i) of MWPSC Act, 2007.
18   S. 5(1) of MWPSC Act, 2007.

or under consideration[19]. Thus, the legislature has done away with many formalities that are usually associated with a normal civil procedure so as to facilitate the elderly group.

The parent or the senior citizen, as the case may be, are allowed to file the application in the district where he resides or last resided[20]. The other option available to the applicant is to apply with the tribunal in the resident district of the children or relative. The tribunal, after receiving the application, shall begin the process of procuring the presence of respondents – the children or relative as the case may be – against whom the application is made[21]. The tribunal is endowed with the powers of a First-class judicial magistrate[22] to secure the attendance of the respondents. After serving notices to the respondents, the Act has made it mandatory for the tribunal to refer the application to a conciliation officer. The officer in turn has to submit his findings of his effort within a month. If an amicable settlement has been arrived at as the fruit of hard labour of the officer, then the tribunal shall pass an order to that effect[23].

4.3.2. Quantum of Maintenance

Section 9(1) states that the tribunal may, on being satisfied with fact that the children or relative have neglected the applicants, may order the respondents to make a monthly allowance for the maintenance of the senior citizen. The section has provided with the tribunal the discretionary power to decide the quantum of allowance. It can direct the children to pay same to the senior citizens from time to time. Section 10 of the Act states that if there is a change in the

---

19 S. 5(2) of MWPSC Act, 2007.
20 S. 6(1) of MWPSC Act, 2007.
21 S. 6(2) of MWPSC Act, 2007.
22 S. 6(3) of MWPSC Act, 2007.
23 S. 6(6) of MWPSC Act, 2007.

circumstances, the Tribunal can effect an alteration in the amount of maintenance. The Section 12 provides an option for the dependants to choose the welfare Act under which they would like to claim their maintenance. For instance, a parent can claim maintenance either under Section 144 BNSS from his children or under the 2007 Act, but not from the both. In case of childless senior citizen, they do not have the luxury of claiming maintenance under BNSS. However, they are eligible to claim maintenance under this Act from his relative or any other person who is likely to have possession or already in possession of his property, as in described under Section 2(g).

4.3.3. Right of Legal Representation

Section 16 of the Act provides a right to a parent or senior citizen to appeal against the order of the tribunal who might have been aggrieved by such order. They are required to file the appeal within the sixty days from the date of order of tribunal. Section 17 of the Act prohibits both the parties from seeking the help of a legal practitioner to represent them either before the tribunal or appellate tribunal. In order to assist the senior citizens in the matters of representation to tribunals, the Act adviced the states to appoint a maintenance officer[24] who is either the District welfare officer or any other officer not below his rank. The maintenance officer is authorised to represent the parents, if they desire, before the tribunal or the appellate tribunal[25].

4.3.4. Old Age Homes and Medical Support

Section 19 of the Act mandates the state governments to establish and maintain old age homes for senior citizens, each housing a

---

24 S. 18(1) of MWPSC Act, 2007.
25 S. 18(2) of MWPSC Act, 2007.

minimum of one hundred and fifty indigent inmates. Section 20 of the Act has made provision for providing medical support for senior citizens. The Act has made provision for providing sufficient beds in government hospitals for senior citizens.

4.3.5. Transfer to Be Void

If the transfer of the property was, done after the commencement of this Act, under the condition that the beneficiary shall provide the basic amenities and physical needs to the senior citizen and when such beneficiary fails in his obligations and renege on the terms of the condition, the transfer shall be deemed to have been made by fraud, coercion and undue influence and shall be declared void at the insistence of the senior citizen[26].

Thus, the MWPSC Act is a welcome relief since the abandoned elders are not required to dawdle through the maze of complicated judicial system and jump through the unnecessary hoops and loops of the same for a relief, but ultimately finding themselves in the same place where they started. The objective of this very comprehensive Act is to provide more effective provisions for the maintenance of parents as well as senior citizens who are not able to maintain themselves from their earnings or properties owned by them. Biological and adoptive parents, step fathers and step mothers are included in the list of beneficiaries. Sons, daughters, grandson and grand daughters are made liable to take care of the elderly. The Act also makes provisions for establishment of old age homes in every district across the country and makes an attempt to provide geriatric care to the aged people.

---

26 S. 23(1) of MWPSC Act, 2007.

CHAPTER – 5

Conclusion

Old age is the foundation of all wisdom and virtues and source of all purusharth aspirations viz dharma, artha, kama and moksha as enunciated in Vedas. The immensely rich cultural heritage of this country has profound influence on all features of its society. And that includes way of living also. The developments are aimed to be practical which shall lead to transforming this society into an ideal one. The ancient Indian society was so modelled for development in all spheres of life with a stress on taking care of the well being of elders. Wisdom and knowledge gained over ages are the reasons for this practical viability. The elders who were driving force behind the transformation of the society needs to be recognised of their importance. Going back to ancient root is one way of handling the issues faced by the elders of today. Way of living is attitude and perception of the people and their society towards life and existence including their reaction to those perceptions. It may include their food habits, social behaviour, religious activities and even economic activities. The Hindu scripts expound that life is sacred and eternal. It is not the physical body that it is taking about, but the soul which is considered to have no death. When life particles interact with the pancha boothas, the five basic elements of the universe and material elements, the birth and death recycles occur. Various religions have different concepts on life. But the crux all these religions are love, tolerance, sympathy and finally salvation. Another common theme that runs throughout these religions is their emphasis on the deference towards the parents and elders.

During ancient India, different dharmas were earmarked to different people. They were aware of their specific duties to be performed during various stages of life. Every way of living has its own strength and flaws. Indian custom had immense understanding of this and it followed various traditional ways to make the life smooth. The main feature of the Indian culture is that every community has strong and inherent support system for their constituents. The elders play a pivotal role in synchronising within these groups guiding the younger generation in their all round development. In Indian tradition till a few decades back, elders enjoyed unassailable power over their children. The three strong pillars of Indian culture are the family, faith and respect to elders, outside of religion. These three are part of virtues that every Indian chose to follow during ancient times. Virtues are high social moral standards that the people aim to attain and lead their life accordingly. And the people are imbued with these virtues by their upbringing right from their childhood. It is not far from the truth that the practice of revering others is what one learns from the elders. It can be further stated that the said moral quality is an inherited one and carried on to next generations. This practice of traditional habitude of deference depends upon the cultural ethos and also what one inherits from their forefathers.

The grey hairs and stiff joints of the elders do not wipe off the wisdom they carry and if the society cares to lend an ear, they are willing and eager to impart their hard gained knowledge to the next generation. The fact that they are the bedrock of the society is undeniable and their importance can be carried beyond babysitting, storytelling and cooking. They are the guardians of the traditions and preservers of a rich cultural heritage. They are repositories of acumen and discernment, a result of a vast experience that will serve as a pharos to the next generation. However, as time evolves, attitude and perception on elders is an ever changing phenomenon. Honour and care taking of elders vary from culture to culture and periods of time. During British colonisation, things however turned to worse. The social structure which remained almost unchanged for many centuries and the Indians' perceptions about way of living underwent rapid changes. It is the still prevalent trend in the society. Aged parents rightfully deserve a fragrance of love and respect. Nothing can be as painful as being abandoned by the children during their second childhood. The youth have to be impressed with the notion that they need not forgo their conviction or sense of self. They will be able to hold on to their creed while simultaneously respecting parents and elders. That is the wonderful feature of Indian culture. Unfortunately they did not and still do not realise this.

The ageing parents look forward the interaction with their children and grandchildren. This adds a touch of colour to the dreariness they might experience at the end of their life. Keeping them aloof will render the elders to create crevices within themselves to hide their emotions which may impair the relationships. It will be a vast vacuum of life, no doubt, when the isolated trudged through monotonous days. We have come across some unfortunate instances where one of the parents has deserted his children as a result of which the children refusing to take care of the parent during his old age. True, there would have been serious errors in their judgements and the whole family would have suffered due to that. But it does not turn them unlovable. After all, we had seen good men have committed terrible mistakes in their life and who doesn't? Even the virtuous Dharmaraj, the senior most of the Pandava brothers have blundered and the whole of the epic revolves around that mistake. A single mistake or a single trait should not be allowed to define the character of a person. Once we recognise the fact that world is not divided into good and bad people, but into good and bad decisions, our battle with our closest will come to an end. We may not be able to change the facts, but surely we can change the way how we react to it. We cannot judge a person until we walk in their shoes. We need to accept and find a closure for the past, take our lumps and keep moving on. It may not be wise to keep retreading the old ground. Destiny sometimes punches us below the belt. But it does not have to prevent us from taking the high road to fulfil our duties. Serving our parents and grandparents is repaying our debt to them. They went to great pains in giving this birth to us, raise us, educate us and to settle us comfortably in life. A selfless & unmitigated affection, absolute care, ceaseless efforts, untold sacrifices for the children and having their back at all times that see their children through many lean and difficult periods are the virtues of parents and elders. Hence it is a duty to take care of them during their dotage in every possible way even if we have to endure sacrifices, difficulties and obstacles.

On the other hand, there is an immediate need to amend the Indian constitution for the inclusion of special provisions for the elderly and bring it within the ambit of fundamental rights. It should be ensured that benevolent measures to the elderly should not be denied on the grounds of mere hyper technicalities. Any slightest infraction has to be dealt quickly and effectively and any knavish tricks need to be frustrated. It is no time for the government to preen itself on its efforts and achievements since there is much more to be accomplished. It is time to develop new innovative strategies, rather than clinging on to button down policies and to make suitable, rather than cosmetic, changes in our approach to address the issues of the elderly, especially their rights. A fair and meaningful solution to the issues of the senior citizens has to be developed so that they spend the rest of their lives productively, effectively, purposefully, satisfactorily and serenely. Instead of providing piecemeal succour to the parents, the government should go for full monty. Even today, in spite of having attained old age, they are capable of making significant contribution to the society and the country, if given an opportunity and it will be an apposite tribute to their experience. The children might have abandoned the parents and elders, but the wisdom they have gained over the years of experience still remain with them. The leaves might have shed, but the tree still grows. The society can use their experience and wisdom for its betterment. It is necessary that the approaches, strategies, planning, policy making and enforcements have to be suitably modified to harness the rich and experienced human resources of the elders for the benefit of the society as a whole. This will ensure the involvement of the aged in nation building and also will result in their inclusion within the society. This will secure their rightful place in the society and improve their satisfaction with the life and mental wellbeing. A large scale participation and engagement of the elderly in the socio-economic development of the society will put an end to their sense of isolation. Also, any monetary compensation for their services will boost their economic independence, thereby improving their standard of living as well as augmenting their confidence to face their issues better. It would be an eclectic mix of fulfilling the necessities of elders and enabling them to perform their obligations. The past had reserved great participation of elders in social and cultural milieus and the people reached their zenith, socially and politically, during their old age. It was a privilege accorded to their experience, knowledge, insights and wisdom gained over the years. It is important that their broods realise that. It is not sufficient if we have ethics alone, but need to have morals too. Else we are no better than animals. By despising all that has preceded us, we let the future generation to despise our self. A perfect place for the aged in the society has to spring from the four walls of their home. When they go bed at night, they should not feel that they survived another hard day. The society has to let them age gracefully since ageing is not just about living longer, it's about living better.